THE
HEROIC
HEART

THE HEROIC HEART

—

AWAKENING

UNBOUND

COMPASSION

—

Jetsunma Tenzin Palmo

SHAMBHALA

Shambhala Publications, Inc.
2129 13th Street
Boulder, Colorado 80302
www.shambhala.com

Verses throughout from *The Heart of Compassion: The Thirty-Seven Verses on the Practice of a Bodhisattva* by Dilgo Khyentse Rinpoche, translated by the Padmakara Translation Group (Boulder: Shambhala Publications, 2007). Used by permission.
Verses from *The Eight Verses for Training the Mind* by Geshe Sonam Rinpoche, translated by Ruth Sonam (Boulder: Snow Lion, 2001). Used by permission.

Cover art: calligraphy by Tashi Mannox
Cover design: Daniel Urban-Brown
Interior design: Kate Huber-Parker

9 8 7 6 5 4 3 2 1

First Edition
Printed in the United States of America

Shambhala Publications makes every effort to print on acid-free, recycled paper.

Shambhala Publications is distributed worldwide by Penguin Random House, Inc., and its subsidiaries.

Library of Congress Cataloging-in-Publication Data
Names: Tenzin Palmo, 1943– author.
Title: The heroic heart: awakening unbound compassion / Jetsunma Tenzin Palmo.
Description: Boulder: Shambhala, 2022.
Identifiers: LCCN 2021038864 | ISBN 9781645470557 (trade paperback)
Subjects: LCSH: Compassion—Religious aspects—Buddhism.
Classification: LCC BQ4360.T45 2022 | DDC 294.3/444—dc23
LC record available at https://lccn.loc.gov/2021038864

THIS BOOK IS DEDICATED to all those who sincerely wish to make their lives meaningful and of benefit to themselves and others. May these words of advice from a bodhisattva such as Thogme Sangpo resound throughout all time and cultures and strike at our hearts, inspiring us to develop a good heart and cultivate loving awareness throughout our lives. The world is in dire need of such goodness.

CONTENTS

Acknowledgments   ix

Introduction   1

1. Making Life Meaningful   11
2. Abandon Attachment and Aversion   19
3. Benefiting from Solitude   26
4. Remembering Impermanence   31
5. Valuing Good Friends   34
6. Relying on Spiritual Teachers   37
7. Going for Refuge   44
8. Valuing Virtue   52
9. Recognizing the Truth of Things   58
10. Valuing Others   62
11. Practicing Kindness and Compassion   70
12. Embracing Adversity   78
13. Bringing Suffering onto the Path   85
14. Not Retaliating When We Are Harmed   88
15. Respecting Even Our Enemies   94
16. Showing Kindness When We Are Wronged   97
17. Respecting Those Who Disrespect Us   102

18. Being Compassionate When Things Are Difficult   110

19. Recognizing What Is Truly Valuable   113

20. Giving Peace a Chance   118

21. Dropping Greed   127

22. Embracing the Nondual   133

23. Recognizing the Illusion   148

24. Letting Go of the Illusion   156

25. Practicing Generosity   167

26. Practicing Discipline   171

27. Practicing Patience   175

28. Practicing Diligence   177

29. Practicing Concentration   182

30. Practicing Wisdom   186

31. Examining Oneself   189

32. Abandoning Criticizing Others   192

33. Not Profiting from Dharma   194

34. Giving Up Harsh Speech   197

35. Cutting Negative Emotions   199

36. Being Mindful   202

37. Dedicating on Behalf of Others   208

Notes   213
Suggested Further Reading   217
About the Author   219

ACKNOWLEDGMENTS

Any book such as this depends on so many interconnecting causes and conditions. My first debt of gratitude is to Atisha Dipankara, who spread these teachings on mind training (*lojong*) in Tibet in the eleventh century. Through him came the Kadampa lineage to which belongs Thogme Sangpo, the author of these present verses. Thence to all the masters who passed down this teaching into the present day. Then I am grateful to the wonderful staff at Deer Park Institute in Himachal Pradesh for inviting me to give the commentary that was the basis for this book over a weekend there some years ago. Deer Park offers a wonderful service to the Dharma by inviting teachers from all traditions to share their knowledge impartially.

The oral commentary, which provided the basis of this present text, was then devotedly transcribed by my longtime friend Arya-Francesca Jenkins. Arya has transcribed so many of my talks over the years, and I am deeply indebted to her for all her skilled efforts on my behalf. Subsequently I edited this transcription for reading purposes but otherwise did nothing about it. However, in time, both Nikko Odiseos and Casey Kemp of Shambhala Publications made overtures about a new book, and I suggested my talks on lojong since this is such a vital and helpful subject for these troubled times. Then in late June 2020, as a wonderful birthday surprise, Dr. Dallas John Baker (Pema Düddul), who is a professor of writing, editing, and publishing at the University of Southern Queensland, offered his expert services in editing some of my talks for publication. This was surely a gift from Tara! So we decided on this commentary on *The Thirty-Seven Verses on the Practice of a Bodhisattva* since it covers a lot of material and offers plenty of practical advice for daily life. The final revision of the commentary from our side was carefully carried out by the American nun Tenzin Dasel.

The text we rely on here was translated from the Tibetan by the Padmakara Translation Group and previously published in *The Heart of Compassion: The Thirty-Seven Verses on the Practice of a Bodhisattva* by Dilgo Khyentse Rinpoche. Each chapter of the present commentary opens with a verse from the translated text. We are sincerely grateful for the permission to use Padmakara Translation Group's translation.

Finally, I thank all those at Shambhala Publications who have made this book possible due to their belief in the perennial importance of these lojong teachings. I remain in awe of the kindness of so many good people in helping to bring this book to fruition. My own part seems so minimal.

THE
HEROIC
HEART

INTRODUCTION

All experiences are preceded by mind,
*   have mind as their master,*
are created by mind.
—*The Buddha*

THE QUOTE ABOVE, by the Buddha himself, demonstrates that our minds and the way we use them, how we think, are central to the Buddhist path. Therefore, a method for taming or calming the mind, a way of training it out of its many negative habits, is both crucial and beneficial. Why is it so important to train and tame the mind? Why is it imperative to release the mind from its habitual patterns and uncover its true nature? Because a wild mind tends to harm others. This brings us to the true heart of Buddhism—the liberation of all sentient beings from all forms of suffering. Although we Buddhists talk about realization and enlightenment a lot, that is not our true goal. Our true goal is to free sentient beings from suffering, to free them also from delusion and ignorance of their true nature. Our own enlightenment is the best and surest way to equip us to do that. It is this cherishing of others that is the essence of Buddhism. From the simplest foundational practices to the heights of Mahamudra and Dzogchen, nothing is more important or higher than the selfless expression of boundless compassion, or *bodhichitta*. Training and taming the mind is the way we give rise to this boundless compassion, and the way we are ultimately able to express our true nature.

We are about to explore an important text on lojong that provides just such a way to tame and calm the mind. The Tibetan word *lojong* literally means "mind training," but the practice really has more to do with training our attitude, training us out of the habitual ways that we respond to situations that happen to us, especially adverse circumstances. The idea is that we take everything onto the path. Some people think that when things are going well, we are healthy and happy and everything is on the up and up, it is a good time to practice Dharma. But when we are faced with adverse circumstances—difficult people, bad health, and so forth—then somehow our practice gets dropped or postponed.

These lojong teachings are about how to take everything, especially adverse circumstances, onto the path. How to use everything that happens to us as a means of inwardly maturing and becoming spiritually strong is the essence of lojong practice. I sometimes compare this to a visit to a gymnasium. The trainer looks at us and says, "Well, your arms are not bad, but your legs are very flabby." So we go on the machines and work out. The reason to work hard on those machines is to become strong. We don't resent those machines because they challenge us. If they are too easy, we find more difficult equipment. We recognize that the effort we make on these exercise machines is the reason we now have nice, strong legs. Lojong is rather like that. The fourth-century bishop of Milan, St. Ambrose, referred to the Christian book of Psalms as a "gymnasium for the soul." There is also the idea that life itself is a gymnasium of the soul. Even though we don't believe in souls in Buddhism, the idea is a good one. Life is where we have our workout, this is where we train. We shouldn't avoid challenges or only work out on the easy machines.

This kind of attitude and these lojong teachings were taken to Tibet in the eleventh century by a great Bengali scholar called Atisha Dipankara Srijnana. Atisha studied this kind of thinking in Sumatra for about twelve or more years with the master Serlingpa.

Then he came back to India and became the chancellor of the large monastic college of Vikramashila. Later, he was invited to Tibet, and although he felt he was too old, he had a vision of the Buddha Tara, who advised him that if he went he would benefit many sentient beings, even though it would shorten his life. Cherishing the well-being of others above himself, Atisha agreed to go to Tibet and had an enormous impact.

Buddhism at that time was going through a lot of confusion about how to put the teachings into practice. Atisha saw that advanced tantric teachings were probably not so appropriate for the kind of minds Tibetans had in those days. What they needed was to get back to the basic principles again and work on their attitudes and motivation. He clarified the path of practice, giving emphasis to the importance of refuge in the Three Jewels (Buddha, Dharma, and Sangha) and on bodhichitta, the aspiration to attain enlightenment for the sake of all beings. Along with providing that clarification, Atisha gave teachings on how to take the vicissitudes of life onto the path, how to approach everything through the lens of cherishing others, of bodhichitta. His followers likewise carried on this tradition, which we now refer to as the lojong tradition, or mind-training tradition.

The lojong text we are discussing here, *The Thirty-Seven Verses on the Practice of a Bodhisattva*, was written in the fourteenth century by a monk named Gyalse Thogme Sangpo, who was born in 1296 or 1297 near Sakya in western Tibet. From an early age he exhibited great qualities of compassion and caring for others as demonstrated in a story from when he was just a toddler. At that time, children wore fleece-lined *chubas*, long jackets tied at the waist. One winter Thogme went out, and when he came back in he was naked. His parents said to him, "What have you done with your chuba?" and he said, "Oh, there is a being out there who was cold." They went and looked outside and there was a bush that was covered in frost. Thogme had put the chuba over it to keep it warm.

Thogme Sangpo's biography is full of these charming stories of how, even as he grew older, he went to immense trouble for the sake of others, especially those who were in difficult circumstances such as beggars, poor people, and so forth. When he was twenty-nine Thogme took full monastic vows. He was an exemplary monk in every way, maintaining his vows with purity until the end of his life. Acutely aware of the suffering of others, including animals, he never wore animal furs or skins, despite the freezing Tibetan climate he lived in.

Thogme became quite learned and served as the abbot of several monasteries. He was extremely well-known and beloved in his day. He died in his seventies. At that time in Tibet people didn't live long, so it was a good age by Tibetan standards. He wrote many books, but the one that has become a classic in Tibetan literature is known as *Gyalse Lalen*. *Gyalse* literally means "children of the Victorious One," meaning bodhisattvas, and *lalen* means "a way of practicing." It is usually translated as *The Practices of a Bodhisattva in Thirty-Seven Verses*.

Our nuns at Dongyu Gatsal Ling (DGL) Nunnery study this text because it is accessible to anyone—monks, nuns, and laypeople, whether Buddhist or non-Buddhist—and because it deals, as all lojong texts do, with how to bring the difficult circumstances in our life, our own mental defilements that give us so much trouble and the problems caused by others, onto the path. It is a practical text because it teaches us how to make use of those difficulties by transforming them and taking them on the path. At first it might not sound practicable for us but, actually, it is highly practical because it deals with how to take adverse circumstances and use them as our practice. This is important for everybody.

I received a commentary on this text from the Sixteenth Gyalwang Karmapa and also a short explanation by the Fourteenth Dalai Lama himself. I also received teachings on this text from Dilgo Khyentse Rinpoche, and I will be drawing on his commentary throughout this book. Most of the verses are fairly self-explanatory, but it is always helpful to receive teachings on them to deepen our understanding.

To complement our discussion of Thogme Sangpo's text, I shall refer to another lojong text, *Eight Verses for Training the Mind* by Langri Thangpa (1054–1123 C.E.), a revered Kadampa master and a shining light in the lojong tradition. I shall intersperse the discussion of this text with commentary on *The Thirty-Seven Verses on the Practice of a Bodhisattva* when the themes of the two texts closely overlap. This way, we will get a deeper understanding of the lojong tradition and a clearer sense of how to apply the teachings in our daily life.

Each chapter of this book opens with a verse from *The Thirty-Seven Verses on the Practice of a Bodhisattva*. The text we rely on here was translated from the Tibetan by the Padmakara Translation Group and previously published in *The Heart of Compassion: The Thirty-Seven Verses on the Practice of a Bodhisattva* by Dilgo Khyentse Rinpoche.

As in most traditional texts, *The Thirty-Seven Verses on the Practice of a Bodhisattva* starts with the invocation explaining for whom the text was composed. Thogme Sangpo starts by saying "Namo Lokeshvaraya." *Lokeshvaraya* means Lord of the Worlds, which is another name for Avalokiteshvara, also known as Chenrezig or Kuan Yin. Avalokiteshvara is the bodhisattva of compassion, who is an appropriate object of obeisance for a text dealing with the bodhisattva's way of compassion. While texts dealing with philosophy, logic, and so forth invoke Manjushri, the bodhisattva of wisdom, texts that deal with the heart and how to incorporate compassion into our daily lives invoke Avalokiteshvara. The text reads:

> Though he sees that in all phenomena there
>   is no coming and going,
> He strives solely for the sake of beings.[1]

"Phenomena" here is translated from the word *dharmas,* meaning ordinary things, just outer things. As we all know, in Buddhism there is a great emphasis on impermanence and the momentary nature of all outer and inner phenomena, on the fact that everything arises and disappears each moment, like a flowing river. It looks like the same river, but moment to moment the water is changing, moving, swirling, and flowing ever downstream. Everything is like that, everything comes into being and disappears again, instantaneously, although in our perception it looks like there is a continuity.

Since impermanence is a fundamental axiom of Buddhist thought we might ask why the text says, "he sees that in phenomena there is no coming and going." Here it is dealing with ultimate reality. In our ordinary, relative way of seeing, things come and they go, things are up, they are down, things last for a long time or they disappear swiftly. But in ultimate reality all these dualities no longer pertain. There is no coming and going, there is no higher and lower, there is no annihilation or endless existence. All these opposites, all these dualities, are transcended in a state of how things truly are. Although Avalokiteshvara is the bodhisattva who represents compassion, his compassion naturally arises from the point of view of his perfect wisdom.

Images of Avalokiteshvara show him with a thousand arms, which represent his endless compassionate activities on behalf of all beings. In each of the thousand hands there is an eye, which symbolizes that he sees the situation accurately, from both ordinary and transcendental levels. Avalokiteshvara knows how to act, or how not to act, because sometimes it is better to leave matters alone, even though we would like to change them. Avalokiteshvara sees things with the total clarity of an enlightened mind; therefore he sees that on an ultimate level there is no coming and going, that all dharmas are in a state of *suchness,* which is beyond the temporal idea of the constant flow of phenomena.

The first line of Thogme Sangpo's text praises Avalokiteshvara's wisdom; the second line relates to compassion. Avalokiteshvara sees the transcendent, the ultimate, while constantly striving for the sake of others on a relative level with compassion. It is important that wisdom and compassion come together; if we don't see things clearly or fully understand the situation, we can mess things up. Avalokiteshvara sees things vastly and just how they truly are. From that infinite perspective he is able to spontaneously act in a way that is of ultimate and relative benefit for beings. By combining ultimate and relative truth, he is also the sublime teacher, meaning our root guru. You could think of His Holiness the Dalai Lama or the Gyalwang Karmapa, both of whom are considered to be emanations of Avalokiteshvara.

To the sublime teacher inseparable from Avalokiteshvara,
    the Protector of Beings,
I pay constant homage with respectful body, speech, and
    mind.[2]

In Buddhism we have the three doors: body, speech, and mind. We pay homage to the teacher with these three. Why? Simply because our teacher is inseparable from Avalokiteshvara. Dilgo Khyentse Rinpoche said in *The Heart of Compassion*, his own commentary on the *The Thirty-Seven Verses on the Practice of a Bodhisattva*:

The sublime spiritual master is inseparable from Avalokiteshvara, the embodiment of the compassion of all the buddhas. Although he manifests in infinite ways for the sake of beings, and displays countless different forms, Avalokiteshvara's nature never changes. Fully enlightened, he has actualized primordial wisdom. His mind is the non-dual, unchanging enlightened mind of all the buddhas—the absolute, Dharmakaya.[3]

The buddhas and bodhisattvas are not separate from our teachers nor from us. They are our true nature—who we really are, if only we could see clearly. We think we are ordinary sentient beings, but we are not. This is our tragedy. But the teacher, a genuine realized being, or lama, is not inherently different from us, and so in Buddhist meditations we absorb either the deity or the lama or both together into ourselves, thinking that our minds and their minds are mixed together like water with water so that we *recognize* that there is no distinction. The distinction comes from our side. We think we are ordinary and they are special, but that's part of our delusion, and so we have to work away at that conceptual distinction, cleaning and polishing. It is like a beautiful silver pot that is so thickly tarnished that it looks black. We have to keep polishing until we get back to the silver which has never, in its essential nature, been tarnished.

However much outer guck there might be around it, if we diligently clean the pot then it will shine. This silver pot was there all the time; it doesn't go away and come back when we clean it. It is always there, but we don't recognize it. All we see is the black covering. Whereas the great *mahabodhisattvas* and the lamas, the true genuinely realized lamas, are very much in contact with their silver base. They do not have that tarnish the way we do because they have already done the work necessary to polish it up and maintain its innate shine. But their essential nature is the same as ours. This is important to remember.

> The perfect buddhas—source of happiness and ultimate
>   peace—
> Exist through having accomplished the sacred Dharma,
> And that, in turn, depends on knowing how to practice it;
> This practice of the bodhisattvas I shall therefore now
>   explain.[4]

The buddhas, like Shakyamuni Buddha, on a relative level, had to strive for countless eons to clear away the tarnish and come back to their true metal. How did they do that? How did all the buddhas of the universe become buddhas? They became buddhas by actually practicing the Dharma. It is important that we practice and take it to heart rather than merely read about it. This is why this text is so important. It is not high philosophy that we need to go away and think about, that is all up there somewhere in the sky. It is absolutely down to earth, which we can all use, all day with whomever we meet. In fact, only by meeting people can we truly practice.

Making Life Meaningful

Now that I have this great ship, a precious human life,
*   so hard to obtain,*
I must carry myself and others across the ocean of samsara.
To that end, to listen, reflect, and meditate
Day and night, without distraction, is the practice of a
*   bodhisattva.*

SAMSARA IS SOMETIMES DESCRIBED as a wheel, but it is also often likened to an ocean. Just as an ocean has large, powerful waves and dangerous tides, so in samsara we are tossed up and down endlessly. Sometimes we are up, sometimes we are down. Then we are up again and then down again. It is just endless. The problem is that we are caught in the waves and continuously thrown up and thrown down. We get battered by life. Let us remember that all these waves going up and down are on the surface. If we go down into the depths of the ocean, we come upon whole realms of calm and quiet, with all sorts of fascinating fish and marine animals and monsters of the deep.

But since mostly we are living our lives on the surface, tossed up and down by our thoughts and emotions, what do we need? We need a boat because, even though a boat also goes up and down, it keeps us from becoming completely drenched and will gradually carry us to the other shore. The Buddha himself many times talked about the other shore, and that other shore is liberation. But we can't just swim because it is too far, and we will get tossed up and down too much and possibly drown. Therefore, we need a boat to cross the ocean of samsara.

As we find in Shantideva's analogy of the boat of gaining human birth in *The Way of the Bodhisattva*:

Cross the sea of emotions
On the boat of human existence.[5]

Now we have this great boat, which is the Dharma, but it is also this precious human life, so hard to obtain. Every single one of us has a precious human birth. We might think, *Well, billions of people have a precious human birth, so what?* But it is not true. A precious human birth does not mean just being born as a human. There are many other factors in the context of Buddha Dharma that make a precious human birth: being born in a Buddhist country or place where Buddha Dharma is still accessible, having all our faculties, having faith in the Dharma, finding a teacher, and so forth. We are not born in the higher realms where everything is pleasant and there is no incentive to practice, and we are not born in the lower realms where there is so much misery and suffering that we are completely caught up in our own paranoia. Nor are we born among the animals who, lovable as so many of them are, do not have the ability to really practice the spiritual path in this lifetime.

What makes a human birth precious? For a start, we can read, and that's an amazing thing in this world. But what is even more remarkable is that we can actually comprehend what we read most of the time. Even though we may not be able to read all the Buddhist texts and know exactly what they mean, we can pick up a book on Dharma and, providing it is not too obtuse, we can get something out of it; the words have meaning. Certainly, if we pick up an ordinary book on basic Dharma practices or biographies of lamas or other great teachers, we can understand them easily and curl up with them and understand the content. We can understand concepts that we have read about but not experienced directly. The mind can grapple with ideas and contemplate them.

Here our text says:

To that end, to listen, reflect, and meditate
Day and night, without distraction, is the practice of a
    bodhisattva.[6]

Well, day and night without distraction might be a bit much, but we have to study.

But back to this theme of a precious human birth. What makes this human birth so precious? Say we are born in a country where we are allowed to think what we want. Consider how many countries in the world would not allow us to think what we want or just go and change our religion or read books on religion or go to Dharma centers. In many countries of this world, either there are no Dharma centers and the word *Buddha* is never heard, or there are Dharma centers but you are not permitted to go because you belong to another religion. This is much more common than we might think if we live in countries like India, the United States, the United Kingdom, or Australia.

So we have our human birth, we are relatively healthy, and we can think, our minds are clear. We have the freedom to think what we want, to read what we want, and we have an interest in Dharma. That is the most important of all. Do you realize how rare that is? How many people are really interested in any Dharma, not just to get the gods to make their children healthy and pass their exams and get more money and a better job, which is mostly what people pray to the gods for, but in the sense of really wanting to transform themselves?

How many people go to the temple to pray for enlightenment for the sake of all sentient beings? How many people even go to the temple to pray for the well-being and happiness of others outside of their family circle? Even to have some aspiration outside of our own self-interest is rare, very rare.

I was brought up as a Spiritualist and every week we had séances at our house. At that time, I was around seven or eight years old. Even at that young age I noticed that everyone wanted to get in contact with someone who had died, and they asked these spirit guides things like, "My aunt Edith is having an operation next week, is she going to be all right?" I thought, *Here we've got these people on the other side; let's ask them something of meaning. They might know or they might have a different angle on it.* I asked them, "Well is there a God?" I thought they might know. The spirit guides replied, "Well of course we don't really know, but what's going round in the spirit realms is that God isn't a person, but ultimately there is light and love and intelligence." So I thought, *Yeah, I'll buy that.*

Ultimately there is light and love and intelligence in this universe. And we are it. It is not just something out there; we carry it within us. This is what we are trying to reconnect with, our original light and love and intelligence, which is who we really are. It is important not to get so distracted by extraneous things but to really remember why we are here on this planet and to realize why having this human body is so precious so that we do not waste our life again. Otherwise we are living basically like a well-trained animal. What do animals want to do? For instance, our dogs at the DGL Nunnery want to be fed, they want to be comfortable. When it is cold they snuggle up in the sheltered places, and when it is warm they lie in the sun. When it gets too hot, they lie in the shade again. They are always seeking comfort. They want to eat nice food. If they've not been neutered, then they want to mate. If a strange dog comes by who looks threatening, they will fight them to preserve their territory, but if it is one of their doggy friends, then they will play around together.

Well, if we lead our lives basically on that level, we might as well have come back as a pet dog. In fact, in New York there are more pet shops than there are beauty parlors! Pets have become like children really. All these pets with their little bows, their little tiaras, and their little jackets. Anyway, the point is, if all we want is to be comfortable and petted, loved and admired, then we might as well have come back as a poodle because we have wasted our human birth. It is hard to get a well-endowed human birth that has the freedoms and the advantages. If we waste this opportunity now, it will be difficult to regain it in the future. All the causes and conditions have come together because of our past efforts in other lifetimes. If we don't make an effort to create the right causes and conditions in this lifetime, we are going to lose the opportunity. Now is the time because we don't know what the future holds.

Now, the Dharma is here, the teachers are still here, the books are still here. We have the freedom to listen and practice; nobody is stopping us. If we don't make full use of this opportunity right now, then next time, who knows? Even later in this life, who knows? The only time we can be certain of in our lives is right now, so this is important.

What we have to do is "listen, reflect, and meditate." First, we have to accumulate the knowledge, we have to listen to the Dharma teachings. Traditionally, in the Buddha's time, things were not written down, so in the sutras they always talked about listening because they didn't have books. The first thing we need to do is listen. This includes reading, studying, downloading off the internet, all of that; any acquisition of knowledge is considered listening.

Listening means to study the Dharma. We take it in, we read about it, and we hear about it, but then we have to think about it, to "reflect" on it. It is not enough that we just take it in. It is like food: we take a bite but then we have to chew it in order to digest; we don't just swallow it in great big lumps. We have to think about what we have read, what we have heard, and really try to understand. If we have doubts, that's fine, no problem. We do not have to believe blindly. The Dharma says that we have to believe because we understand. If you don't believe something then put it aside for a while or go study more.

Almost every year when I was staying in Lahaul[7] I would go and see my lama, the former or the Eighth Khamtrul Rinpoche, and I always had a long list of questions from my retreat. I used to keep a piece of paper beside me so that when a thought or a question would come up I could write it down and forget about it rather than keep it going in my mind. Then when I went to see my lama he would lean back and say, "Where's your list?" and I would bring out the pages with all my questions. I think Rinpoche kind of enjoyed it because the questions went up and down and all over the place and occasionally he said, "Oh, nobody ever asked that before. I have to think, hmmm."

There were some things about Tibetan Buddhism I really didn't believe, and he would say, "It doesn't matter, just put that to the side for now." Sometimes he would laugh and say, "Everything you read in the books isn't true." Once he even said, "Well we just write like that to frighten people into being good!" The point is that one doesn't have to believe everything. We need not be frightened that a thunderbolt from heaven is going to come down and hit us if we don't believe everything. It is not like that. What we need is an intelligent belief, a belief based on our own reasoning.

Sometimes I call Buddhism "enlightened common sense" because once we hear it, we think, "Yes, that makes sense." But if we hear or read something and think, "Hmm, that doesn't sound right," then we put it aside or maybe study more about it. Maybe we didn't understand it or maybe it was just a provisional truth that isn't ultimate truth anyway. Perhaps it was just what people believed in society at that time. We don't all have to believe that the world is flat with Mount Meru and the four continents, but that is the kind of cosmology that was current in those days. Nowadays nobody gets burned at the stake for believing that the world is round. The world is round, the world is flat; in any case, it is all empty! Think things through, really try to understand. If you don't understand, then read more about it, think more about it, ask questions. Reflection is a crucial part of the Dharma.

Then, most important of all our text says, meditate. But actually the Tibetan word *gom* literally means "to become accustomed to or familiar with something." What we have to do then is practice it, put our ideas into action. One of my lamas said, "First you hear and study, then you think about it, then you become it." And that's the point. It goes from the head down into the heart, and we transform. Then spontaneously what we say, what we think, and what we do comes naturally from our understanding.

This is very important, because otherwise mere learning is not going to help us. I once went to see Trijang Rinpoche, who was a key tutor of His Holiness the Dalai Lama. His first question of course was, "Who is your lama?" I said, "Khamtrul Rinpoche," and he replied, "Ah, Kagyu! Well the thing with the Kagyupas is that they practice, that's the emphasis with the Kagyus." Then he turned to his secretary and said, "At the time of death, what is going to help us, a head full of book knowledge or genuine understanding and realization in the heart? You know, we don't need to study so much. What we need is to study, understand what we have read, and then really practice it and put it into our heart. That is what is going to help us."

Without practice and understanding in our heart, studying is just endless learning, learning, learning while nothing inside is transforming. If someone says something nasty to us, and we get all upset and defensive and think, *How can they do this to me?* then what is the use of all this learning? We haven't learned anything.

These three things are very important. First we have to study to know what we are trying to do, then to really think it through so that we really understand it, and then incorporate it into our lives and become it. We've got work ahead.

Day and night, without distraction, is the practice of a
bodhisattva.

This means whatever is happening, even if it is just occurring in
a movie we are watching, we should try to see it from a Dharma
point of view. For instance, if the movie is supposed to be a ro-
mantic drama, with attachment, jealousy, and anger being acted
out, we should be observing it with clarity of mind and openness
of heart. Day and night, we are constantly practicing the way of a
bodhisattva. Dilgo Khyentse Rinpoche noted the following with
regard to this verse:

> Every day, remind yourself that if you do not study and reflect
> upon the teachings, meditate, and recite prayers and mantras,
> at the moment of death you will be helpless. Death is certain.
> If you wait for the moment of death to begin your practice,
> it will be too late.[8]

There is no time off if you are a bodhisattva. It is twenty-four hours,
seven days a week—what can I say?

2

Abandon Attachment and Aversion

*In my native land waves of attachment to friends and kin
    surge,*
Hatred for enemies rages like fire,
*The darkness of stupidity, not caring what to adopt or avoid,
    thickens—*
To abandon my native land is the practice of a bodhisattva.

THIS SECOND VERSE does not just refer to our outer native land.
It doesn't just mean that we all have to go across the world in order to practice, because we take our mind with us, and it is our
mind that has all this attachment and hatred and the darkness of
our unknowing.

On the one hand, people get locked into habitual relationships.
Dilgo Khyentse Rinpoche put it this way:

> The meaning of leaving behind your native land is to leave
> behind the emotions of attachment, hatred, and the obscuring
> ignorance that permeates both. These three poisons, generally
> speaking, are most active in the relationships you establish
> with family and friends in your own homeland.[9]

How often people react to each other out of old habits, without
even really thinking about it anymore. So many negativities come

up because of the way people habitually act and talk to others with whom they are familiar. Maybe the patterns started in childhood, and they continue on and on.

On the other hand, it is good to be able to get away and maybe get some new perspective through being in a different environment where we can try to incorporate better ways of dealing with people. But the problem really is that "native land" means our ordinary habitual responses; these are what we have to leave behind. And the way to leave them behind is first to be conscious of them.

The waves of attachment surge within and around us. We are lost floundering in this huge ocean caring about people and worrying about them and fearing they are going to leave us and then becoming happy again when they tell us that they love us. Parents with their children, couples in relationships, all of this; there's so much going on that it is rare to be able to relax in calm quiet waters. Mostly the waves of our hopes and fears send us surging up and down. It is all our attachment. Attachment doesn't mean love; there's a huge difference between love and attachment. The Buddha said the cause of our suffering, of our *duhkha*, is attachment, clinging and grasping.

But love and compassion, which are essential qualities on the path, are quite different. They are actually the opposite of attachment and grasping. This is one of the most difficult distinctions for us as ordinary sentient beings to really understand because in our society we believe that the more we are attached, the more loving we are. But it is simply not true. Attachment is tricky, but basically it means "I want you to make me happy and to make me feel good. Conversely love says, "I want you to be happy and to make you feel good." It doesn't say anything about me. If being with me makes you feel happy and good, wonderful; if not, then so be it. The important thing is that love allows us to hold things gently instead of grasping tightly. It is an important difference.

As an example, I tell the story of my mother. My father died when I was two, so he was out of the picture, and my mother brought up my brother and me by herself. Eventually my brother joined the Royal Air Force in Malaysia, so only I was left at home, and my mother and I got along very well. She was also interested in Buddhism, so we would go to Dharma meetings together and entertain whichever lamas or monks were in London at that time.

Then when I was nineteen, I got a letter from India telling me that there was work for me and to come. I remember running through the streets to meet my mother who was coming from work and saying to her, "Oh, I am going to India!" And she replied, "Oh yes, dear? And when are you leaving?" She didn't gasp, "You're going to India? How can you leave me, your own poor mother? I'll be all by myself with no one to take care of me and look after me as I'm getting old!" She never said any of that, not because she didn't love me, but because she did love me and wanted what was right for me, even if it did not include her.

Afterward, when I was in India, every ten years she would write, "If I send you a return ticket, will you come back for a month?" and so every ten years, I went back for a month, spent time with my mother, and then returned to India. She also came to India for one year. She loved India—it was very different from the way it is now, but she loved it. She loved it, she loved the Indians, loved the Tibetans, but she got sick from the food so she had to go home to England. But that was love.

There's an Australian cartoonist named Michael Leunig who did a series about how to respect and show love for others. One of his examples was holding a day-old chick in your hands. You hold it carefully, gently, because if you grasp it—no more chick! Love is like that.

Love is an outpouring of caring and wishing the other to be happy, but not with you stuck right in the middle of it. Not grasping, *I want you to be happy but only if it includes me.* Because we get so caught up with our families, and it is hard not to be attached to family, the second verse uses the example of leaving the homeland.

However, it doesn't necessarily mean that we have to leave home. What it does mean is that we have to start thinking in a different way about our loved ones—a way that genuinely cherishes them and wishes them well but allows them to be who they are without trying to manipulate them or make them say and do what *we* want them to do because that would make us happy. It's about allowing them to be who they are and giving them the freedom to have *their* life, whether or not that includes us.

So we start by practicing on those we love and are close to. We practice how to genuinely love them, as they are, whatever they are, without grasping. I remember when I was fifteen or sixteen my mother one day out of the blue just said to me, "I want you to know that there is nothing you could ever do that would cause me not to love you." That's love. I wasn't doing anything, but I appreciated the thought, and I knew it was true. Whatever I did, my mother was there for me but without trying to manipulate, just allowing me to be who I was and loving that.

Another problem is that if we are continually in our ordinary environment, it is easy to cultivate antipathies and conflicts; some may have even begun in childhood. We like this person, but we don't like that one. It is easy to feel long-term hostility toward our neighbors or even our siblings, when we have not examined why we feel the way we do. It is hard to see people who we know well, like our family, as they really are and not as our projection.

So it is helpful sometimes to just step back and look at people who are very familiar to us as though we had never seen them before. To just drop all our preconceptions, all our ideas, all our opinions and just see them, without any kind of judgment at all. Listen to them. Hear them as if for the first time. See them as if for the first time, afresh. We get locked into our habitual reactions and judgments, with usually too much attachment or with antipathy. Even people who love each other are often locked into a hostile way of reacting that they don't examine. They spar with each other all the time, and they don't hear each other. It is like one of those soap operas that are endlessly being rerun. Why not change the channel?

So this is what it means to leave one's homeland. It doesn't just mean physically removing ourselves, but much more importantly, it means inwardly shifting to a different space. This is so important and why this advice comes near the beginning of the practice. To really start seeing things from a different angle as if we were in a new place, meeting new people for the first time, and seeing them with affection and the wish for their happiness. Basically, just seeing people with no prejudgments.

Another helpful practice is to step back and just hear oneself speak. Not judging, just listening. The tone of voice. The kind of language we use. The way we speak and what we say. So often we are not even conscious anymore. It is so automatic. How we speak to one person compared with how we speak to another. Just listen. We don't hear ourselves. Often if someone plays back a recording, the person speaking doesn't recognize themselves. They don't know their own voice. "Oh goodness, do I sound like that?!"

We can try to see things anew. It is important to look at our mind and to start clearing out a lot of the junk and debris which we carry around with us as if we were in an old attic. We sort through all the junk and think, "Why on earth did I keep all that?" We can start throwing stuff out and cleaning up a bit. Especially concerning our habitual responses. Because the lojong teaching is all about how to cultivate skillful responses in place of our habitual unskillful responses. We need to look and question and see without pretending. We need to cultivate inner change. Where we see something in our responses which is not helpful, which is negative, that is our path. That is our practice. To change and transform. Everything can be changed.

"The darkness of stupidity" refers to the fact that the whole problem is that we just don't see. Why do we get so obsessively attached to other people? Why do we get angry with people who don't do what we want them to do? Why do we keep doing and saying the wrong things when we know it is stupid? Why do we not do the things we know would be helpful? Ultimately it is because of this darkness of our own unknowing, but also because of our habitual inertia. It is so much easier to go along with the way we've always done things. It takes such a lot of self-awareness and effort to change.

Even though we know that going along the way we have been going doesn't lead to anything that we want and just creates more problems. Still, there's this heaviness when it comes to actually making the effort to change. This is like a thick fog which comes into the mind and prevents us from seeing with clarity: what could be done differently, what would be skillful and what is unskillful. Even if we've read about it a thousand times, we still find ourselves caught up in the same old habitual responses.

To change physical habits is a challenge, but to change mental and emotional habits is even much more of a challenge. Nonetheless the good thing is that it is possible. Nowadays neuroscientists are busy mapping out the brain, and the good news is they say that we can indeed create new neural pathways. We can also slowly close down old neural pathways. Our minds and behaviors are not set in stone. The brain is quite pliable. It can change. It is like a river that flows in a certain direction but can be diverted somewhere else.

Likewise, we can make new channels. We can create new pathways. Imagine a forest with a familiar path that we always use. After a while this path becomes well worn, compacted and clear so we know exactly where we are going. But now we don't want to travel on that road anymore. For instance, somebody says something unkind and we get all upset, angry, and hurt—which is just the ego being sad that people don't love it.

We don't want to go on that unprofitable road that doesn't lead anywhere. We want to go on this new road of skillful responses, but there isn't yet a road. We have never before tried this new road of thinking, "Well, thank you, I'm glad that you're so horrible because now I can practice patience." We don't have a road in our brain for that one, so we have to create one. We start to go along this new road, but then the grass springs back and it doesn't look like we ever went that way before. But if we keep going along this same path every day, eventually we will create a road.

Then gradually the grass and flowers start pushing up through the old pathway that seemed so permanent, and after some time, we don't see a pathway anymore. The new way has become the pathway. But this only comes from repeated effort. It doesn't happen overnight. It just doesn't. Anyone who promises that it is all effortless is just deceiving you, because these habits are deep inside our psyche, like thick, deep roots. It takes a lot of conscious awareness and effort and determination to transform. But the good news is we can all change. Of course we can. As the Buddha said, "Yes, we can change. If we could not change, I would not tell you to do so, but because you can, I say for goodness' sake get on with it," or words to that effect.

But it is important to remember that nobody, not even the Buddha, can do it for us. It is up to us. Teachers can help. They can guide and they can encourage, but they cannot do it for us; if they could, they would. We must accept that we are responsible for our own heart-mind, even though other people are there to help us—either by being kind and encouraging or by being absolutely awful and obnoxious. Either way, they are genuine spiritual friends, as the text will explain.

We recognize that these three poisons inside our heart—our attachment, our hatred, and our basic unknowing or ignorance—are the cause of our suffering in samsara. It is not out there; it is inside us. We can do something about it. This is the whole message. We don't need to discard anything thinking it is an obstacle to practice. In fact, everything is a help to our practice if we have the right attitude. It is a matter of changing our responses. That's all.

3

Benefiting from Solitude

When unfavorable places are abandoned, disturbing
  emotions gradually fade;
When there are no distractions, positive activities
  naturally increase;
As awareness becomes clearer, confidence in the
  Dharma grows—
To rely on solitude is the practice of a bodhisattva.

WHEN SPEAKING ABOUT THIS VERSE, Dilgo Khyentse Rinpoche said, "When you live in a solitary place, your negative emotions gradually diminish, and your self-control and moderation increase."[10] These texts were written for monks and hermits who typically live in solitary places, but we can also understand this in a deeper way. It doesn't just mean outer solitude. It also means an inner solitude. "When unfavorable places are abandoned, disturbing emotions gradually fade." The point is, what are "unfavorable places"?

The foundation of Buddhism is renunciation. In Tibetan, the word for renunciation is *ngejung*, which means "to really get out of something." If we are serious about becoming the masters of our minds, instead of the slaves of our emotions; if we are dedicated to leading a life that will be of benefit for ourselves and others, then we have to be selective. We cannot do everything in this lifetime. We cannot spend all our nights partying and then get up at five in the morning to do our practice. Well, we could, but it wouldn't work very well. We have to decide in our lives what is really important to us and what is not. Then simplify. This is renunciation.

Renunciation is looking at our life and our activities and recognizing what is counterproductive to our spiritual path—what is a distraction and what encourages the growth of the negative emotions and discourages the growth of positive ones. Then we can decide that we are not interested in going along with that anymore. In English the word *renunciation* conveys a sense of gritting our teeth and giving up something that we really want but know we shouldn't have. When I was eighteen and became a Buddhist, I gave up Elvis Presley. I gave away all my records and magazines thinking that was a renunciation. But that's not really what renunciation means.

When we are young and we have favorite toys like a teddy bear, we take that teddy bear around with us everywhere, and we really love teddy. Even though teddy is dirty and scruffy and he's lost an eye, we love him. If someone tries to take teddy away from us, it hurts. Something in our heart is torn out. We are not ready to give up teddy. But as we get older our interest in our children's toys fades away. We are just not interested anymore. We've replaced them with computer games, or whatever. But we've shifted our object of desire. We've got different interests. Now if we lose our teddy bear, so what? We've outgrown him.

As the wonder of the Dharma takes over our life more and more, we lose interest in other things that previously had seemed so important to us. It is like the leaves of a tree in the spring and summer when the tree is in full bloom. If we try to pull the leaves off the tree, there's a resistance because the leaves are firmly attached. But in the autumn, the attachment eases and the leaves naturally just fall. They fall because they are getting ready for new growth.

Similarly, as our interest and involvement in the Dharma deepens, our involvement and interest in so many other worldly distractions naturally fades away. We are striving to grow up and become adults, in the true sense of the word. The Buddha called ordinary people caught up in worldly distractions "the childish." We are trying to mature. Often the path is called *mindrol.* The word *minpa* means "to ripen, to mature," and *drol* means to be liberated, to be free. We have to ripen or mature our mind stream in order to be liberated.

When the instruction says, "When unfavorable places are abandoned, disturbing emotions gradually fade," it doesn't just mean moving to a different country. It can also mean changing outer circumstances that don't serve us, like endlessly watching television or looking at the computer or mobile phone, drinking and partying, or just talking a lot of useless gossip and worldly talk. Those situations create a lot of disturbance in the mind. Therefore it is beneficial to avoid those kinds of activities and instead frequent places where people are interested in more spiritual topics, such as Dharma centers or anywhere that has a positive atmosphere. We should associate with people who are kind and have good values and talk about subjects that have some genuine meaning. These are good places where one's negative emotions begin to subside.

As much as possible, we should look for environments where the afflictive emotions such as our anger, aggression, jealousy, and attachment begin to grow less. At the same time, our good qualities are given a chance to increase because everybody else is trying to be kind and friendly, and so naturally one wants to be kind and friendly too. It becomes natural when we are in an environment where these qualities are admired and appreciated.

It is also important to be selective with the company that we keep. Later on in the text it talks about avoiding bad company. What it means is that as ordinary sentient beings, we are influenced by the society around us, usually much more than we would like to admit. Unless we are careful, we often take on the values of the people with whom we habitually associate. Therefore if we are with people who are only thinking about worldly distractions and worldly aims, then gradually, bit by bit, our interest in the Dharma could begin to subside, and our fascination with outer things begin to increase. Even though we don't intend it, it just naturally happens like that.

So we have to be selective. This doesn't mean that we are rude to people who don't want to meditate for six hours a day, but it does mean we should closely associate with people who basically have the same kind of values and appreciation for the Dharma life. Even if they're not Buddhists, they should at least be genuinely good people. As they say, if we put even an ordinary piece of wood in a sandalwood box, then it will take on the smell of sandalwood. But if we bury it in a dung heap, then, of course, it will smell like dung. We should be careful.

As we begin to practice and our minds begin to calm down and our innate virtue begins to appear, our appreciation for the Dharma deepens. Nobody adores the Dharma in the way that the great realized masters do. They hear just one word of Dharma, and their eyes fill with tears, even though they've heard the same thing a million times. Because they know how precious the Dharma is: they have not just studied it, they have not just thought about it, they have become it. Their appreciation and devotion is genuine, so they are deeply grateful.

When our minds gradually begin to see more clearly, with less delusion, less judgment, and more clarity, and all our upsets, anger, and ego defenses begin to quiet down, then our incredible gratitude to the buddhas—and all the masters who came later and have preserved this precious lineage—just spontaneously arises in the heart. Our faith is uncontrived. When we imagine a world—and our lives—without the Dharma, we feel deeply grateful. Deeply grateful.

While the practice of abandoning unfavorable places and allowing disturbing emotions to fade is not necessarily easy, it is certainly possible. As we go through each of the practices in turn, we find that the text is actually describing the four thoughts that turn the mind away from ordinary worldly activity and toward the Buddha

Dharma. These four thoughts are a powerful practice in themselves and entail:

1. Contemplating our precious human life so that we are grateful for our existence.
2. Contemplating impermanence and death so that we seize the opportunities of this life right now.
3. Contemplating karma, or the law of cause and effect so that we understand that our every action impacts ourselves and others.
4. Contemplating the suffering of cyclic existence (samsara) so that we are no longer entranced by worldly things.

We have already discussed the precious human birth and how lucky we are to be here with all the endowments that we carry with us. The second is impermanence, which we will consider next.

Remembering Impermanence

Close friends who have long been together will separate,
Wealth and possessions gained with much effort will be left
*   behind,*
Consciousness, a guest, will leave the hotel of the body—
To give up the concerns of this life is the practice of a
*   bodhisattva.*

OF COURSE, THIS VERSE goes completely against the mentality of our modern consumer society, which is so centered on this life and how happiness depends on close relationships, success, money, possessions—the more you have, the more you are. The text points out that our consciousness is just a guest in a hotel. This body is only here for a short time. However long life lasts, in cosmic time it is less than a finger snap. Then the guest has to leave and find another hotel. In other words, absolutely everything is impermanent. This includes ourselves. Furthermore, all the stuff that we've accumulated has to be left behind for somebody else, even if our whole life was spent gathering and accumulating. At the end, no matter who we are, we don't take one single coin with us, nothing. However many loved ones and friends, disciples or groupies you have around you, not one of them can go with you. You're all alone. Naked. The only thing we carry with us is our karmic imprints. And what have we done about that? Dilgo Khyentse Rinpoche points out the following:

Ordinary, worldly concerns bring only suffering and disappointment in this life and the next. The appearances of samsara are highly unstable, ever changing, and impermanent, like lightning as it flashes across the night sky. To reflect on the impermanence of all phenomena helps turn your mind toward the Dharma.[11]

Recently I read an article that was written by a woman who had spent many years taking care of hospice patients and people who had drawn-out terminal illnesses. She made a number of observations that were fairly common with all of them. One was the tremendous transformation as they accepted that they were going to die, which most people don't ever want to think about. They acknowledged that death was there. Of course we are all going to die. We don't have to be a cancer patient to know that. But normally people don't want to think about it. Now these patients had to think about it.

This transformed their lives because they began to recognize what is important and what is not important. One of the major regrets was that they had spent so much of their life working so hard to accumulate all their possessions—big houses, more cars, an important position in their company, and so forth—instead of giving more time and energy to what was really important, like spending more time with their children and with their partners, concentrating more on spiritual issues, and doing things that have real importance in this world. They had been lulled into believing that what really mattered was getting on in life. That was the primary regret everybody had, which is interesting.

Many of them also felt happy that they had some time to say they were sorry to people that they had hurt and to tell their loved ones that they really loved them. They just reevaluated their whole life, and what was important was more about what they had done for the world than about what the world had ever done for them.

One of the good things about Buddhism is that it talks a lot about death. This is important because by talking about death, it reminds us that we are alive and that we need to assess what we are doing with our life because we are not going to have it forever. We can appreciate something if we know we are going to lose it. If we think we've got it forever, then we don't value it anymore.

When I was a little girl, I used to think that we were all on a train journey and that the train was going to crash, only we didn't know when. Why were we wasting our time just gazing out the window and going to sleep? Why weren't we doing something more important with the short time we had before the train crashed? I can't remember if I did anything about that, but that's how I used to think.

It is important to recognize that even the closest people who have been together with us since the beginning are one day going to separate from us and we don't know when. Just because we love somebody doesn't mean that we can stay with them forever. It is not possible. Where are the people for whom in our last lifetime we would have given our life because we loved them so much? And in the next lifetime there will be a whole new cast.

We spend so much time trying to cultivate relationships that are precious while we have them, but we should make them as harmonious as possible because they will not last forever. Also worldly possessions will definitely be left behind. We have to recognize that whatever we have gathered we leave behind. We take only the karmic seeds, our *samskaras*, our habitual mental patterning, with us. But we are usually careless about the karmic imprints in our substratum consciousness. And yet, that's our wealth. That's what we can take with us.

Right now our whole future, not just this lifetime but future lifetimes, is being decided. It is in what we do with our mind, with our speech, with our body. Moment to moment to moment we are creating our future. Nobody else can do it for us. Therefore, how we choose to spend our time, on practice or on frivolity, and who we choose to spend our time with, are clearly of paramount importance.

5

Valuing Good Friends

In bad company, the three poisons grow stronger,
Listening, reflection, and meditation decline,
And loving-kindness and compassion vanish—
To avoid unsuitable friends is the practice of a bodhisattva.

AGAIN WE COME BACK TO the fact that we are easily influenced, and if we hang out with the wrong set of people, we start to take on their attitudes, and we want to be part of the group. Dilgo Khyentse Rinpoche explains that:

A crystal, when placed on a piece of cloth, takes on the color of that cloth, whether white, yellow, red, or black. In the same way, the friends with whom you keep company the most often, whether suitable or unsuitable, will greatly influence the direction your life and practice take.[12]

We begin to imitate and get into bad habits. We know very well that among young people one of the reasons that so many get into drinking, drugs, and promiscuous sex and so forth is not necessarily because they are really that interested. It is because they want to be part of the gang. They want to belong. Therefore, they get in with the wrong crowd and down they go. It is hard then to pull out. Sometimes they end up addicted or in serious trouble. So we have to be careful. The Buddha himself said that good companionship was essential on the path.

As much as possible we try to be with people who inspire us, whose example we want to follow since this will increase our virtues and help decrease our negative emotions. Otherwise it is difficult. Obviously if our family is not particularly spiritually minded it doesn't mean we have to ignore our whole family, but it does mean that we don't have to take up their values. For example, if our family are all heavy meat eaters, and we want to be vegetarian, we become vegetarian. We don't have to eat meat just because they're eating meat.

When I was in Italy, I was in a large hospital, and I said I was a vegetarian. They had never heard of such a thing! Then the head chef came up to see me to find out what he could cook. He said, "Well, why are you a vegetarian?" Since my Italian is not good, I said the simplest thing I could say. I quoted Bernard Shaw, who was a vegetarian: "Animals are my friends, and I don't eat my friends." The chef said, "Ah! Si, certo, certo!" and he cooked me delicious vegetarian food. The rest of the ward was so jealous.

The point is that we don't have to adopt the values of others if we think their values are wrong for us. In fact, often if we just carry on acting from our point of view and can explain in simple language why we are doing so, people get interested. They might even follow. For example, when you are a vegetarian, people start to think about it and recognize that actually they are eating animals who want to live as much as anybody else wants to live. Slowly maybe others in the family will become vegetarian or at least cut down on their meat eating. It doesn't hurt them.

If we cannot be an example, then what? Even though we are not buddhas radiating light, if we try to be a person of integrity, honesty, and kindness, people will be attracted to us. We don't even have to say a word. People will be drawn to us. This question of how easily we are influenced by the company we keep is important. As much as possible we try to associate with friends whose values and way of life we truly appreciate and honor. They aren't necessarily Buddhists or even on any particular spiritual path, but they are good people. Then we begin to emulate that.

We should be careful of people who may appear to be nice and friendly but have values that are wrong for us. People who are only thinking about money, physical comfort, food, or intimate relationships might be charming, but we have to be careful. We are like tiny saplings that need protection from strong winds that can come along and destroy them. This process has to be nurtured, protected, and fertilized. If we start spraying it with noxious chemicals, then it is finished. These negative ideas and thoughts are like poison.

Sometimes it might look like the fruit is big and beautiful, but actually it has no taste and it is lifeless inside. At the nunnery we test our food with a pendulum. Of course, coffee and sugar and so on were negative, but we also tested the apples and oranges and carrots. For the big beautiful-looking carrots there was either no movement or it swung in slightly negative direction. Then when we tried some organic products, the pendulum swung around enthusiastically in a big yes.

So even some things that look outwardly fine actually have no essence. They have no value. Outer beauty but nothing inside. Like roses nowadays: they look beautiful but have no scent. Like those gourmet carrots that look beautiful but have no taste and no nutrition. Likewise, we should be discriminating with the company we habitually keep because we can be in a group where people look good and prosperous, everything's going okay on the outside, but then actually inside there is nothing. Of course we should be friendly to everybody, not heavily judgmental but discerning. Because we are easily influenced, we should strive to be affected by what is good and worthwhile. This brings us to verse 6 on spiritual teachers.

6

Relying on Spiritual Teachers

Through reliance on a true spiritual friend one's faults
will fade
And good qualities will grow like a waxing moon—
To consider him even more precious
Than one's own body is the practice of a bodhisattva.

WHERE VERSE 5 DEALT WITH people who are bad company for us, this verse deals with good friends. The ultimate good friends are like the buddhas, the bodhisattvas, and one's spiritual teachers. They are obviously the kind of company we should hang out with. But "true spiritual friends" doesn't just mean those kinds of people. It also means other companions on the path, whichever path they're going on (if it is a good path), and who therefore demonstrate for us genuine goodness.

His Holiness the Dalai Lama again and again talks about cultivating a good heart, and this is what we are trying to do here. Therefore we should try to associate as much as possible with people who are good hearted because they remind us how to act in situations where we are not feeling very good hearted. Then we can improve ourselves again. This is about changing and improving. We have to surround ourselves—or at least associate whenever possible—with people who exemplify what we are aiming for and remind us of how it can be.

It is helpful to be with people who value the things we value and are sincerely striving toward overcoming their negative qualities and cultivating positive qualities. It is especially helpful to associate with those who are much further along the path than we are who will be a big inspiration for us.

Why do so many people love the Dalai Lama? Because he so completely exemplifies what a genuine human being should be—what everyone wishes they could be. He's a man not only of great wisdom and compassion but also of great integrity. As he walks by a line of people, he looks into their eyes, and he takes their hand for two seconds, and their lives are transformed. Because in that moment not only have they met with a genuine bodhisattva in the flesh, but they have been looked at by someone who totally accepts them as they are and loves them unconditionally. Whoever they are, they know that. His Holiness doesn't care who you are. He just looks straight into your buddha nature and acknowledges that. That's why even a brief encounter is so powerful, even though they only meet him for two seconds. We can be with other people for hours, and feel nothing particularly significant, but His Holiness and the great lamas or other spiritual beings of that caliber have a great effect on people because they are so genuine.

The Buddha said, "What I think I say, and what I say I do. This I can say for myself." Such perfect integrity! As much as possible, we should not only try to exemplify that in our own life but also associate with good friends, because they will always remind us of our own potential and where we are going. Sometimes when we just read these things in books, they all become a bit distant, far away. But when we actually see somebody who embodies these qualities, then we recognize it is possible for us as well—they're human beings, I'm a human being. Why not?

When the Tibetans in exile first arrived in India, there were many great lamas who had been trained in Tibet and were quite traditional. They didn't speak English, and most of the Westerners who came to see them at that time didn't speak Tibetan. There wasn't much you could do. You just sat there. But that was all that was needed. People would meet these masters and think, "Well I don't know what you believe, but I'm going for it," because these lamas were the personification of a perfect human being. Here was the embodiment of our own great potential sitting in front of us, smiling away. Not saying anything. Not doing anything. Just being. And that was enough.

Many Hindu devotees have the custom of *darshan*, which means "seeing." In darshan you go into the temple, and you sit there and look at the guru. The guru doesn't do anything. They just sit there, being the guru. If it is a genuine master, then that is enough. But there are a lot of charlatans too.

"Through reliance on a true spiritual friend one's faults will fade, and good qualities will grow like a waxing moon" means that if we are under the guidance of a genuine teacher, then that teacher will help by pointing out our faults and encouraging our virtues. They might not necessarily speak about our faults, but in some way they will create situations where our faults come to the surface and we can see them. In that kind of nurturing atmosphere it is like being in a hothouse where plants will grow much better because they are in an environment set up to be conducive for their growth.

But even if we don't happen to have any particular spiritual teacher at this time, we can still cultivate meeting with people who are an inspiration and who genuinely embody the teachings. And even if we don't have a personal relationship, just being in their presence can be helpful. Again, on a more relative level, we can also try to be selective with our ordinary friends and (as much as possible) to be with people who share the same values. Because otherwise, as I say, we get badly influenced and can get ourselves into a lot of trouble.

The spiritual teacher in Tibetan Buddhism is considered important because, as with any skill, if we want to learn properly, it is better to have a teacher. If we want to be a musician, learn football or cricket, or understand computers, it is obviously better to have a trained teacher who can tell us what to do and what not to do. Not only does it make learning quicker, it also prevents us from picking up all sorts of bad habits we are not conscious of and that later down the road will create a big obstacle to really mastering our skill. Whereas, if at the beginning we have a good teacher who says, "No, don't do it that way, do it like this" or encourages us when we do things right, we won't make so many mistakes, and we will make much quicker progress. Additionally, we will develop more confidence that we are doing it right.

If this is true for learning practical skills, what about truly understanding and transcending the conceptual mind? We need guidance to intuit the nature of the mind and then to stabilize that realization. We also need someone to keep us from being carried away when experiences come up, and we think we are already enlightened. We need a teacher. Dilgo Khyentse Rinpoche notes:

> All accomplished practitioners of the past attained enlightenment by following a spiritual teacher. They would start their search by listening to accounts of the doings of different masters. When the stories they heard about a teacher were particularly inspiring, they would examine [their] qualities from a distance before committing themselves. Once they had complete confidence in [the teacher], they would go into [their] presence, serve [them], and one-pointedly put whatever instructions [they] gave them into practice.[13]

It is hard to attain enlightenment on our own. Very, very hard actually; we can't just learn from books. Books can get us started and be helpful, and nowadays a lot of teachings can be downloaded off the internet, but this can never replace a personal relationship with a teacher if we can get it. The problem is getting it. Finding teachers who are genuinely qualified is not so easy. Even if someone is a genuine teacher, then they've usually got a whole organization around them to protect them from seeing anybody, and they run around the globe constantly setting up their Dharma centers. It is actually quite a challenge. Many people come to me complaining because they do not have a teacher. Then others come along complaining because they do have a teacher.

So it is difficult, and it can be quite a minefield. But for those who are genuinely serious, it is helpful to have personal guidance on the path if you can find it, because without a teacher it is an incredibly difficult process to turn our ordinary samsaric mind into a buddha mind. In fact, it is almost impossible. But in the meantime, that doesn't mean that we have to sit around waiting for the perfect lama to appear. I often say to people, "With an untamed mind, what can anybody do?" Even if the Buddha himself were sitting in front of us, all he could say is "practice." That we can all do.

Imagine that the mind is like a wild horse. Although it is absolutely wild, it still has potential; it is a good horse. But when we want it to go this way, it goes that way. When we want it to go up, it goes down. Anybody who's sat in meditation for five minutes knows what I am talking about. The mind is like a wild horse, but it has great potential to be trained. However, we cannot train a wild horse without first taming it. Taming it means that it quiets down, becomes trusting and interested in what we want it to do. It becomes friendly, cooperative, and amenable. Then we can start to train it. We can teach the horse to do anything within the capacities of what is possible for a horse once the horse has agreed within itself that it wants to cooperate. But as long as it does not want to collaborate, we cannot train it.

Likewise with the mind. We start with *shamatha* practice to allow the mind to quiet down and become calm and single-pointed. In Tibetan it is called *lesu rungwa*, which means "workable." We make the mind workable, flexible, and cooperative. Nobody can do that for us, and it wastes a teacher's time to wait while we try to get our mind into some kind of condition where they can really teach us. This we can do for ourselves. Get the mind calmed down, more clear, more conscious. Develop the qualities of being mindful and being inwardly vigilant, alert—know what's going on in the mind. Have the power of attention so that if we want to stay here, the mind will just rest here instead of going off everywhere else. This takes time with patience and perseverance. Whether or not we have teachers, all of us can learn to tame the mind. Once the mind is tamed, then it can be trained.

Practicing even the highest yoga tantras (Anuttara Yoga) with a distracted mind is a waste of time. Sorry, but it won't get us anywhere. In order for our practices to work, the mind has to completely merge with the practice and become one with it. Otherwise there's the undertaking of the practice and the mind that is trying to make contact for a few seconds, but then the attention goes off again. This is not going to accomplish much.

So the first step is to learn how to make the mind workable. That alone is a huge step forward; we can do this. Nobody else can do it for us. We all have to struggle with that. However, as one great lama said, "If you have good shamatha practice, then the rest of the Dharma is in the palm of your hands." The mind will merge with what we are doing and become one with it, and the results will come quickly. Otherwise, as the books say—if we don't have a concentrated mind, then even if we recite mantras for a million eons, the results will not come. Which is obvious, if we think about it. Everybody is so interested in all these high practices which we can't do properly because the base is not there. It is like wanting to build a golden roof when there are no foundation and no walls.

Once we have established the foundations and have a consistent daily practice, then we will benefit from the guidance of a teacher who can help us deepen in our practice through their experiential wisdom of the path. There is no point repeating the mistakes many others have made along the way, nor taking unnecessary detours. The teacher helps us avoid mistakes, shows us a direct way forward, and keeps us on track. This is a practical thing. The teacher saves us time and unnecessary effort. Although we still have to walk the path ourselves, it will be much harder without an experienced guide.

7

Going for Refuge

Whom can worldly gods protect
Themselves imprisoned in samsara?
To take refuge in the Three Jewels
Who never fail those they protect is the practice of a
    bodhisattva.

THE PREVIOUS VERSES were basically presenting us with the problem, and now comes the solution. This is the situation we are in, so how do we get out? Again, Dilgo Khyentse Rinpoche summarizes the issue:

> People naturally search for refuge, for someone or something to protect them from sorrow and torment. Some people turn to the powerful with the hope of achieving wealth, pleasure, and influence. Others seek protection through natural forces, such as the stars, or mountains. Some seek aid through the power of spirits. But none of these mistaken objects of refuge are free from ignorance and samsara, and they therefore cannot provide ultimate refuge. Their compassion, if they have any, is partial and limited.[14]

Rinpoche further explains that true refuge can only be provided by "something that is itself totally free—free from the bonds of samsara, and free from the limited peace of a one-sided Nirvana."[15]

According to the teachings, this quality of true refuge is to be found only in the Three Jewels—the Buddha, Dharma, and Sangha—which are considered to have "absolute wisdom, non-biased compassion, and unimpeded ability."[16]

In many parts of the world there are two levels of devotion for the people: there is the official religion, and then there is what most people actually believe in. You see it here in India, for example, in Hinduism, where there are the higher gods such Shiva, Krishna, Saraswati, and so forth, and then there are what are called the local gods.

Himachal Pradesh, for example, is full of local gods who we may or may not see. Every village has its local god. In the town of Mandi at the time of Shivratri (the nights of Shiva) all the local gods, about 150 of them, gather from the local villages into Mandi. All these gods are usually related to each other—they are cousins, brothers, sisters, so they are very happy to see each other. They are carried on palanquins, which resemble stretchers but have poles borne on the shoulders of the male devotees. The deities themselves are just faces made in bronze. Sometimes special ones are in silver. The faces are usually peaceful, occasionally slightly wrathful. The main deities and the attendant deities are wrapped up in silks and brocades. These palanquins sometimes sway and jump around as though animated by the devata. The village men carry long horns that they blow, and sometimes people are dancing. Anyway, these are devatas.

These are the local lower deities who are vowed to protect the various villagers, especially those who have faith in them. Usually the devata has somebody who acts as a medium and channels them, so that people can go to them with questions and problems. They respond and if they can, they give advice, protection, or benefits.

However, ultimately, what can they do? They are themselves trapped in samsara. They can try to give some mundane benefits, if they are propitiated and pleased. They can also get angry. When we first started our nunnery, for the first few years we had several cases of our nuns becoming possessed by the local spirit of their village who did not like them to be Buddhist nuns, and they were really in a bad state.

For example, one nun's mother had experienced a difficult pregnancy with complications, so the family had made offerings to the local devata and, as a result, she was born safely. Then the devata said, "Now she belongs to me, so she should serve me." This girl then had to go to the local shrine and help with the puja rituals. But when she left to become a nun, the local god was upset. He said that she couldn't go to the Buddha because she belonged to him. Then apparently he would possess her, and she would act strangely. And this created a lot of problems. In the end, we had to do a ceremony for propitiating the devata, but finally we sent her back home.

There are a lot of these lower gods, and they are spiritually superior. They may be considered superior insofar as they don't have a body and do have a certain amount of clairvoyance, they are often jealous and proud, and they get angry easily. In fact, they are quite temperamental—attached to those they like and nasty to those they don't like. In other words, they are samsaric beings.

The reason people honor them is because they are easy to contact. It is not hard to build up a relationship with them, whereas it is difficult to make contact with the buddhas and bodhisattvas or Shiva and Vishnu or even Jesus Christ, because they are so far beyond us. It is more difficult to feel their care. Whereas these local deities are quite close to us, so we can have a relationship with them. In Thailand, also, every garden has a spirit house for the local devata, and I'm sure in South America, Africa, or Australia, people have relationships with these entities; it is a worldwide phenomenon. But they are samsaric beings, part of this world system.

Thus to place our refuge—our hopes and trust—in a samsaric being like that is a big mistake, because they cannot help us get beyond samsara. All they can do is sometimes help us, depending on our karma, in worldly matters. There is a widespread practice throughout the Himalayas of propitiating these local spirits. In the region of the Himalayas where I lived for many years, Lahaul, everyone was doing Buddhist rituals, but many people were also performing the shamanic rituals of the local spirits and gods. Therefore, this verse is not just something that was relevant eight hundred years ago but is no longer relevant today. People still rely on practices that are focused on giving quick returns. In comparison, the Three Jewels seem very remote.

But we must remember that the Three Jewels are not just to help us pass our exams or to make our sick relations better. The purpose is beyond that: it is to get us out of samsara. Only beings who are themselves beyond samsara can help us to likewise go beyond. Beings still trapped in samsara cannot do that. As the verse says,

> Whom can worldly gods protect
> Themselves imprisoned in samsara?[17]

These worldly gods are already imprisoned; they are not free. How can they give us the key to get out when they themselves are still locked inside?

> To take refuge in the Three Jewels
> Who never fail those they protect is the practice of a
>   bodhisattva.[18]

"Never fail those they protect" doesn't mean that if we are having trouble with our business and we pray to the Three Jewels, we are going to hit the right market. What it means is that if we sincerely believe in Buddha, Dharma, and Sangha, and we sincerely practice, this refuge won't let us down. Our practice will definitely flourish. Our ability to come closer and closer to a liberated mind will definitely improve. The Dharma—being truth—cannot let us down, but our own practice of it can.

The Dharma itself cannot fail us, because it is how things really are. It won't fail us because the protection that the Buddha, Dharma, and Sangha give is to the mind. How they protect our mind is what is explained in the verses to follow, which are concerned with how to use the adverse circumstances we are likely to meet in samsara and transform them into our opportunities for practice. That's where the mind is protected, because it can never be crushed. Because we have the methods by which we can always surmount, transcend, and transform the difficulties we meet. This is one way that the Three Jewels are a protection for our own mind.

If we sincerely practice from our heart, we will be able to cope with even the most awful thing that could happen to us. In fact, it might be the opening that we have all been looking for. The Buddha himself is not going to appear waving a sword to defeat all our enemies, but if we ourselves transform our mind from within, we won't have any enemies, and in that way, we will be protected.

So the foundation of the Buddhist path is to take refuge. Nowadays many people practice Buddhist techniques, especially tonglen meditation, and they read many Dharma books without actually becoming Buddhist. This is good, because one of the beauties of the Buddhist path is that it can be adapted to individual needs. It can even be used to lower blood pressure, reduce stress levels, and make one feel a bit better. That's wonderful, but that's not what the Dharma is all about.

Dharma does not just make us feel better—in fact, it might make us feel worse initially. But the Dharma helps us to overcome the inner poisons of our mind and to connect with our true nature and to become free. To become liberated, so that we are really able to benefit other beings. It helps us to get beyond this egoistic self-absorption in which most of us are drowning. Although Buddhist ideas can be used as a good therapy, they can also be used as a boost for other people's spiritual paths. Many Christians (including priests and nuns) practice Buddhist meditation, and it makes them better Christians by relaxing their minds, which makes them more open to others, and by igniting compassion and devotion in their hearts. This is wonderful and is why we all rejoice. This helps us become better people and that's what is important.

Nonetheless, from a Buddhist perspective, the first step is the belief and trust in the Buddha, Dharma, and Sangha. What does this mean? Well, traditionally the Buddha is considered to be the supreme physician, the ultimate doctor, because we are all poisoned by our negative emotions, especially our greed and attachment, anger and aversion, jealousy and pride, along with the underlying quality of our delusory lack of understanding: our ignorance. We don't recognize who we really are. We will go into this more later, but this underlying grasping at a false identity—who we are not—and not recognizing who we really are is the cause of all these other poisons. We are sick with afflictive emotions, and that's why we are not always endlessly bubbling over with happiness.

Then the Buddha says, "Yes, you have a big crisis, but there's a reason why you're so sick." The underlying cause is the grasping, clinging, attached mind based on our wrong perception of our identity, which creates a lot of problems. The Buddha said that suffering is birth, old age, sickness, and death as well as not getting what we want and getting what we do not want. In fact, it is the whole quandary of living tossed up and down in the ocean of existence called samsara.

If the Buddha had left it at that saying, "Well it is your problem, because you're grasping too much," then indeed Buddhism would be pessimistic. But, of course, he didn't. He said, "Good news! Ultimately you are perfectly healthy, and what is more, there is a cure!" There is a therapy we could follow and then we would become so healthy, we won't believe it. The therapy is the noble eightfold path which basically encompasses the whole of Dharma. The Buddha is like the doctor.

If we are really sick, we don't want to go to a doctor who says there's nothing wrong with us, because we know there's something wrong, otherwise we wouldn't have gone to a doctor. But if the doctor tells us the reason why we are sick and assures us there is a cure and that if we follow the treatment we are going to be healthier and healthier, then we are grateful to that doctor. Here, the Dharma is the medicine we take that helps to cure us.

The word *Sangha* has basically three levels of meaning. The first is the Arya, or Noble Sangha, which comprises those—whether monastics or laypeople—who actually have had a genuine perception of reality. In the Tibetan tradition this is realization of emptiness or *shunyata*. At that point one becomes an arya, or noble one. That is the Sangha we go to for refuge because they know what they're doing. They are like nurses who have been trained. They are not qualified as doctors, but they have experience and they can help with our treatment.

The second level of the Sangha comprises the monastics, which means all those who are ordained and receive vows as monks or nuns. The third level is the Maha Sangha, or Great Sangha, the fourfold community of fully ordained monks, fully ordained nuns, laymen, and laywomen. The Buddha talked a lot about the fourfold Sangha and said that in order for a country to be a genuine Buddhist country, it had to contain the fourfold Sangha because when the monastic Sangha is combined with the lay followers it is stable like a table with four legs.

One of the arguments for introducing the full ordination of nuns in Tibetan Buddhism as well as in Thailand, Myanmar, and so forth, is that according to the Buddha's own classification, countries are not really considered Buddhist if they only have three of the four constituents needed to make a Maha Sangha. If they don't have fully ordained nuns, they are not, as far as the classification is concerned, genuine Buddhist countries.

Going for refuge to the Buddha, Dharma, and Sangha is a ceremony that has existed since the time of the Buddha himself. Again and again in the Pali canon when people come to the Buddha for discourse and answers to their questions, the text ends by having them say, "From here until life ends, I take refuge in the Buddha, I take refuge in the Dharma, I take refuge in the Sangha." In all Buddhist countries, from the time of the Pali canon until the present day, the threefold refuge is still recited usually at the beginning of any ceremony.

So in Buddhism we take refuge, and this can remind us to place the Dharma at the center of our life instead of at the periphery, only practicing when we have a bit of spare time. We are practicing the Dharma in whatever we are doing. It is not something abstract that speaks of a higher philosophy or the advanced levels of meditation. It is, instead, a beautiful and useful text dealing with the kind of situations, problems, and challenges that come up in everyday life and teaches how to transform them into a Dharma practice by responding in a genuinely skillful way that can help us transform our heart-mind.

As mentioned in the introduction, these kinds of teachings came from Atisha who saw that advanced tantric teachings were probably not so appropriate for the kind of minds Tibetans had in those days. What they needed was to get back to the basic principles again and work on their attitudes and motivation. Therefore he emphasized refuge and bodhichitta. Atisha founded the Kadampa tradition, and subsequent teachers also emphasized these basic principles again and again. It is like a heavy piece of dough that we have to knead continually until it becomes soft and flexible and is ready to be used. Our minds are like that heavy dough, and we need to keep practicing until the mind lightens up and becomes flexible and pliant.

8

Valuing Virtue

The Buddha taught that the unendurable suffering
  of the lower realms
Is the fruit of unvirtuous actions.
Therefore, to never act unvirtuously,
Even at the cost of one's life, is the practice of a bodhisattva.

THIS VERSE DEALS WITH KARMA. Karma is the third of the four thoughts that turn the mind toward Dharma. Now it seems that karma for some people is a problem. Actually I was shocked when I was in America attending a conference of Western Buddhist teachers of all the various schools. At one point the question was asked, "How many of you believe in karma and rebirth? How many believe in other realms of being?" Less than half of these Buddhist teachers acknowledged a belief in rebirth or karma. But if one does not even believe in rebirth, it makes nonsense of the whole Buddhist path. The Dharma is basically reduced to a therapy to make this life more tolerable. With such narrow vision there is no place for bodhichitta.

Simply stated, the Buddhist view is that—at the conventional or relative level—we have all experienced thousands if not millions of rebirths in every possible realm we can imagine. Not just as humans but as animals, in the spirit realms, higher realms, and lower realms. We should remember that if we met ourselves in our last lifetime, we wouldn't know ourselves at all. It is not me that gets reborn.

If we could see ourselves in the next lifetime, who would that be? I would be a completely different being, but that being would also be thinking, me. We don't have to cling too tightly to that personal identity. There is just a stream of consciousness going forward that, as long as we believe in a me, is endless. Somebody once asked, "Well, how can we ever end it, since we are always doing actions with our body, speech, and mind?" The master explained it with a mala, or rosary of beads. Taking a bead, she said, "All right, we do this act, thinking 'I did this' and then that bead pulls the next bead which pulls the next bead; they just keep following, one after the other after the other. So what to do? Well, obviously we need to cut the thread, then we pull one bead but the other beads don't move. They are just left behind. The thread is the belief in an I who did the action."

As long as we believe I performed this, I did this, I said that, then that's the thread that keeps the karma coming along with us. This is important because it is the reason why in Buddhism we can be liberated. Once we realize the emptiness of our false identification with a sense of me and mine—the spider in the middle of the web—then although we may act beautifully and appropriately and spontaneously as buddhas and the great bodhisattvas do, there is no I in the center. Karma is not being made. Karma, or action, depends on an actor. So long as we believe I am doing something, there are seeds being sown, and if we think of all of our past endless lifetimes, we've done everything. Good, bad, indifferent—you name it.

We've taken on many roles in many lifetimes, and all the seeds of our intentional actions of body, speech, and mind have been accumulating in what is called the "substratum consciousness," so when the time comes, when the causes and conditions come together, certain seeds will sprout. We don't know which seeds or when or how. But it is never arbitrary; there are always causes and conditions there—things we did at some point. That's why bad things happen to good people and fantastically good things happen to really awful people. It is not that there is someone up there judging us and meting out rewards and punishments. It is just that at certain times certain things will come up because of past causes.

That we can't do much about. We can do some purification practices, but there are endless seeds to be purified. Perhaps the best purification practice is to take whatever happens onto the path. Moment to moment we are creating our future by how we respond to what is happening in this moment. It is like a tapestry that we are endlessly weaving.

Sometimes, as a result of responding positively to difficult circumstances, we turn what looks like something negative into something positive. From a simplistic point of view, we say "good" and "bad," because we think good is when things go according to our wishes and bad is when they don't. But actually from a more expansive point of view, it is hard to know what is good and what is bad.

Often people look back on their lives and see the times of most difficulty and challenge, like sickness or losing a loved one or being made redundant, and they realize that it was a wake-up call. That was when they found their inner strength to deal with the situation, and looking back later, they can see they learned so much from that time and they are grateful for it now.

During all the good times, although they are nice, one tends to free float and not make much effort to change. It is often harder to take the good times onto the path than the bad times. Therefore even the higher celestial realms are considered to be a spiritual dead end simply because there is no challenge. When everything is already so nice, why bother to strive?

Therefore, when the text talks here about good karma and bad karma, we have to understand this is meant in a conventional sense. Nonetheless, when difficulties come, especially sickness and poverty and the many problems that appear in our lives, they are the result of negative actions that were performed in this life or former lives.

Now those seeds have come up, so we need to respond skillfully and take this on the path. Then that negative karma transforms into positive karma.

I had a friend who was an Australian nun, quite young, and she had breast cancer of which she subsequently died. She said that one time she was sitting feeling very sorry for herself thinking, *Why did this happen to me?* She had led a healthy life and eaten all the right foods, had all the right thoughts, so why was this happening? Then she said she had a kind of waking vision in which she was male and felt she was a crusader, wearing a white tunic with a big red cross, and she was standing over the body of a prostrated soldier, the enemy, and pointing a big sword at his heart. He was begging for his life. She knew she had a choice: she could forgive him or she could kill him. Then she thrust the sword straight down into his heart. She came back into everyday consciousness and felt her question was answered. Now, whether or not it was so, the fact is that through the ages, there are thousands or even millions of people who have killed other people and animals. From a karmic point of view, we have to accept the consequences of those actions.

The important thing is not to worry about what is going to happen to us but to create inner strength to deal with whatever does happen. We will be able to take it on the path with us. Something that outwardly looks negative can inwardly be exactly what we need as a real help and aid to our practice.

This is so important, and it's what this text is all about. It is like going to a gymnasium because we are out of condition. There are all these exercise machines designed to challenge our muscles. If they are too easy, we adjust them to make them more difficult, to make them more challenging; otherwise, how are we going to get strong?

So we practice the Dharma because we need to get strong. It is no good telling ourselves, *Oh this is impossible. I can't do this, I am too weak.* It is because we are weak that we need these texts to help us develop those inner spiritual muscles, so that whatever happens to us, we can deal with it. Then there is no hope and fear because whatever occurs, we can take it on the path.

This is what lojong is all about: developing the confidence and the qualities that will help with whatever happens to us in our lives as our practice. Instead of moaning and complaining and feeling sorry for ourselves, we appreciate that this is our opportunity to practice properly. It is pointless to be a fair-weather Buddhist who practices when the sun is shining but runs for cover as soon as it starts storming.

> The Buddha taught that the unendurable suffering of the
>   lower realms
> Is the fruit of unvirtuous actions.[19]

The lower realms are the hell realms, the realms of unsatisfied spirits, and the animal realms. As Shantideva pointed out in the *Bodhicharyavatara*: "Who created the red-hot floors and the demons who torture the beings there? All these are created by the perverted mind."

We live in a world of our own projections. When we are happy, everything is sunny. When we are depressed, the brightest day is gloomy. Since we have an apparent physical basis (which according to quantum physics is neither physical nor as apparent as we assume), our projections are totally subjective. As humans we are all equipped with certain kinds of sense organs and consciousness so there is a general consensus about how things are, despite the distortions of our emotional reactions. Two people might go to the same place and experience a completely different version of the situation depending on their mental state. But in the nonphysical realms, which include the hell realms, everything depends on our state of mind, which means that we project our psychic state outward and then we react to it.

Actually, if one reads certain sutras, it seems as if for everything we do there is a hell realm. One time I went to my lama, Khamtrul Rinpoche, and said, "Well, it is impossible, for everything there is a hell realm!" Rinpoche just laughed and replied, "Oh well, we just write like that to frighten people into being good!" He said that it is actually difficult to get into the hell realms because they depend on a mind state that delights in cruelty and in hurting others. There are people who take pleasure in evil and the suffering of others, who enjoy inflicting pain. They are far from their original buddha nature. When they die, they project all the darkness and cruelty inside their minds, which returns back to them. Then they react angrily and fearfully, creating more hallucinations in an endless cycle. This is why it is so difficult to get beyond those states. One is trapped in endless paranoia, anger, and fear.

Now the average person is not like that. Most people are basically good-hearted. We have our good qualities and our failings. However, when we die we are likely to encounter circumstances that correspond to our usual way of thinking while we were alive. It is important to be careful what we think about and how we respond to situations now when we have some choice, because this is what we could meet with and experience in the afterlife. We don't want to create more problems for ourselves in the future, so we should be careful of our actions right now while we have a choice. We can decide to avoid doing anything nonvirtuous, even at the cost of our life. *Nonvirtuous* basically means "that which harms others." Just don't harm anybody, with our body, speech, or mind. It makes sense and has unforeseen and profound benefits. Dilgo Khyentse Rinpoche puts it as follows:

> The more careful you are in whatever you do, the easier it is to realize emptiness; the more profound your view, the clearer your understanding will be of the relationship between cause and effect.[20]

9

Recognizing the Truth of Things

Like dew on grass, the delights of the three worlds
By their very nature evaporate in an instant.
To strive for the supreme level of liberation,
Which never changes, is the practice of a bodhisattva.

THIS VERSE, LIKE VERSE 4, is about impermanence. Dew on grass lasts for such a short time; the sun rises, and it is gone. Likewise all these things that we imagine will give us pleasure and delight are ephemeral. Practically speaking, even the most delicious meal in the world is going to end. Then what? We probably get indigestion. Any pleasure that we can think of is short-lived and often hardly worth all the trouble that we went through to get it. Dilgo Khyentse Rinpoche explains it this way:

> All those illusory goals and ambitions, even if you could ever manage to follow them through and bring them to some kind of conclusion, would that lead to a lasting result? You will recognize that there is nothing permanent in any of them. You might be the heir to a throne, but it is obvious that no king has ever maintained his power indefinitely—if nothing else, death will snatch it away. You might be the most formidable general, but you will never subdue all of your country's enemies, no matter how many wars you wage. You might have

tremendous power, influence, fame and wealth, but it is all meaningless and hollow.[21]

One of the problems in our modern society is the idea that happiness means pleasure. Therefore a really happy life will be one of unending pleasure. But actually unending pleasure would be extraordinarily boring and unsatisfactory. Some psychiatrists say that the problem for most of their patients is not any psychiatric issue per se. They don't have psychosis, schizophrenia, or anything like that. Outwardly they are prosperous and seem to have everything, but inwardly their life is utterly meaningless. There is no purpose.

Yes, they got the position in the firm that they wanted. Certainly they have a nice house and family and three cars, and they can buy more or less whatever they want. Yet they ask, "Is this all life is about?" Increasingly, people are experiencing this sense of hopelessness, because they've got everything that society tells them is needed for happiness, satisfaction, and fulfillment—and they are miserable.

Many people now have enough sense to understand that getting another car or a bigger house is not going to solve the problem. That no matter how much they get, beyond a certain level of security and comfort, it's not going to fulfill them. What then? Is that all the struggle is for? People work so hard, struggling like rodents on wheels, endlessly moving and getting nowhere.

This is the malaise of the modern world now. So many people are getting so much and recognizing that it doesn't make them happy. A few years ago I attended a happiness conference. It was set up by a Buddhist organization, but most of the speakers were psychiatrists, sociologists, neurologists, and so forth. The question was, "What is happiness and how do we get it?" I remember one sociologist, who was not a Buddhist, said that it had recently been shown that people have a certain level of basic happiness. That level may vary slightly for different people, but each has a basic level. If, for example, someone wins the lottery, their happiness level goes up for a time and then the next year it returns to that individual's normal level. Or if someone has a terrible accident and becomes disabled, their happiness goes down, but then after a while it comes back up again.

The sociologist said that the only thing they have ever found that raises the happiness level and keeps it raised is meditation, because it gives one an inner joy that is not dependent on outer things. So provided they carry on practicing, they can sustain this feeling of well-being and joy. Otherwise all these delights and pleasures are nice, but they are also transient, lasting only for a short time. We feel uplifted and then go back to the normal drudge again.

So assuming that our happiness depends on outer circumstances is a false trail. Therefore, what is the right way to go? Perhaps we could start on our inner possessions. Not the outer wealth, which at a certain point is counterproductive. I know many wealthy people, but they don't seem especially happy. I also know lots of poor people—some of them are extremely happy, and some of them are not. Happiness doesn't depend on material possessions. When I was living in a cave, I didn't have anything much, not even a torch. Yet I was perfectly happy, so not having anything was totally irrelevant.

It is sad that the more traditional societies are discarding their own standards. They are throwing away their own culture, which gives them an identity and dignity as a people, for the modern "junk" culture, which often depreciates their own long-held traditional values.

Burma, now known as Myanmar, was under a repressive government for many years. Then they tried democracy. Hundreds of political prisoners were released, and Aung San Suu Kyi was in parliament. This was wonderful. Things were relaxing and opening up much more. I got a letter around that time from Burma (Myanmar), and it said that there was music in the streets, and people smiling and feeling more relieved and happier.

But because the situation was opening up, the world sanctions on Myanmar were relaxing, which meant that China, India, the United States, and Europe were all planning to descend on Myanmar and buy up all its wealthy assets, such as rubies, diamonds, gold, and probably oil or natural gas. For a long time, these assets had been frozen due to boycotts of the regime. Now these countries were looking to make trade agreements and flood the country with all their junk products. In addition, tourism was set to boom as Myanmar became the "in" place to visit, which meant big luxury hotels and resorts and tour groups from around the world were planned. Goodbye traditional Burma, goodbye Burmese heritage. Now Aung San Suu Kyi is under house arrest again and democracy is on hold.

Ironically, during the time of the regime, Buddhism flourished. The Dharma flourished, and there were many meditation centers. Laypeople also practiced, and in the evenings the local stupa became the social center full of people, young and old, sitting and reciting their prayers, meditating, circumambulating, making offerings, or just sitting around chatting. But now Myanmar's future is uncertain. One of the few unique Buddhist cultures of the world is just about to take a big fall. This is called impermanence.

10

Valuing Others

If all the mothers who have loved me since beginningless
*   time are suffering,*
What is the use of my own happiness?
So, with the aim of liberating limitless sentient beings,
To set my mind on enlightenment is the practice of a
*   bodhisattva.*

THE FIRST LEVEL OF ASPIRATION is seeing that samsara is impermanent and understanding that outer acquisitions are not going to
make us happy. Since everything is impermanent, we should strive
for liberation or Nirvana. Get me out! When really in the depths of
our heart we recognize the uncertainty, the insecurity in samsara,
no matter where we are, then, like being trapped in a prison house
we search for the key to escape.

I once dreamt that I was wandering through an immense prison.
There were luxurious penthouse suites with people at cocktail
parties, and there were other rooms in which people were working
or talking and laughing or crying. Then, way down deep were the
dungeons where the inmates were suffering, being tortured, and
despairing. But I recognized that regardless of whether one was
up there in the penthouse or down there in the dungeons, it was
all a prison. Those up in the penthouse today could be down in the
dungeons tomorrow. Or vice versa.

It was so insecure, and we had to get out. In the dream I went around saying to people, "Look, we are in prison, how do we escape?" Most people answered, "Yeah, maybe it is a prison, but it is okay." People weren't alarmed. I said, "No, you don't understand, it is so uncertain, we don't know what is going to happen to us, we are all caught in here. We've got to get out!" But people said that either it was all right really or it wasn't worth the trouble trying to escape because there was no way to leave. Eventually I found a few friends who agreed to come with me. There was a boat moored on a stream that ran through the prison, and there were guards on watch, but they didn't try to stop us. We got on this flat boat and floated down through the stream until we got outside the prison.

On the outside there was a road running parallel to the prison, so we started running and running. On one side we could see the prison looming, the high walls full of windows inside of which we could see vignettes of people singing, dancing, laughing, crying, and working. We kept on running.

The prison seemed endless, and I was exhausted. At first I thought, *It is not worth it, let's go back again.* But then I thought, *I'm not running just for my own sake. If I stop running and go back, then my friends who are following will go back too. So, for* their *sake, I have to keep running.* As soon as this thought occurred—as soon as I stopped thinking about running just for myself—the prison ended, and another road appeared running perpendicular to the road we were on, and the dream carried on from there.

Verse 9 deals with striving for the supreme level of unchanging liberation. We are aiming for Nirvana in order to escape from samsara. However, there is a problem here. The traditional example of this is a burning house. The house is on fire, and there is a huge blaze, but we have managed to get out. But our parents, our children, our loved ones, and our cat are still in the burning house. Can we just walk away? No. We have to go back in and try to get them out of that burning house. We wouldn't just leave them inside to burn to death. We would take the fact that we ourselves are out as the reason to help pull them out, too.

Another example is that we are all drowning in the swamp of samsara, but we have finally managed to get onto dry land. Yet looking back, we see our loved ones who are all drowning. Who would say, "You're drowning! Sorry about that, but I'm on dry land, so you take me as an example and swim hard. I hope you can get on dry land too. Bye!"

How would one do that? In fact, one would say instead, "Okay, now that I am on dry land, I must get some rope or use my hands to draw these people out, too. Come a bit closer, I'm going to pull you out!" We can use that firm land to help pull everybody else out. We wouldn't let our mother drown in front of us if we could prevent it. Or our children, our partner, our friends, or anybody. Even a street dog we would try to rescue. Of course we would.

This brings us to the next level of motivation, which was mentioned earlier and is called bodhichitta. *Bodhi* means "enlightenment" or "awakening," and *chitta* means "heart" or "mind." So *bodhichitta* means "mind of enlightenment" or "spirit of awakening." It's that awakened heart quality that helps us to travel the spiritual path, not just so that *we* will feel better, but so that we can help others to feel better, too. Through wisdom and compassion one is in the position to benefit beings in a meaningful way. Dilgo Khyentse Rinpoche taught:

> The bodhicitta of intention, of aspiration, has two aspects: compassion, which is directed toward beings, and wisdom, which is directed toward enlightenment. Neither aspect by itself, either the mere wish to benefit beings, or the mere wish to attain enlightenment, expresses bodhicitta . . . if you do not aim at attaining ultimate enlightenment, then however strong your wish to benefit beings may be, you will never go beyond ordinary kindness and compassion.[22]

This is similar to being sick ourselves and then recovering and afterward seeing other people who are ill. Because of our own experience, we are sensitive others' suffering, and we wish to dedicate ourselves to helping them gain health. Therefore, we aspire to become a doctor. When we gain enough knowledge to graduate from medical school, it is not because we want to cure ourselves, it is so that we can benefit and heal others. Likewise, on the spiritual path our motivation is to be able to understand things more clearly to benefit others. If we could learn to deal with our negative emotions, if we could have a deep insight into the nature of reality, then we would be in a position to really benefit all these other beings who so desperately need to be helped.

Considering how many billions of people there are in the world, it seems that in this lifetime we are connected to just a few. Just our parents, siblings, children, and other family members and the people with whom we come into contact such as friends, colleagues, and so forth. A comparatively small number.

But if we look back through the endless panorama of all our past lives, then how many beings have we actually had a close relationship with? It's hard to say because we have completely forgotten. Even if we meet again, we wouldn't know them anymore. Sometimes we meet somebody for the first time, and they immediately feel familiar to us, as if we've known them before. And other times we can be with people for years, and we still don't feel any particular connection.

From the point of view of opening the heart, the usual focus is on the role of the mother, because frankly without our mother, none of us would be here. It is unfortunate that we don't remember that one time in our life when we were most cared for and nurtured. Anybody who has to take care of children knows that it is a full-time job—especially when the children are small. The mother has to keep up an endless round of washing them, feeding them, changing their diapers, cuddling them, and putting them to sleep. And what do little babies do? They suckle, they shit, they cry a lot, they keep their parents awake at night, and occasionally they smile. They are totally focused on their own needs and wants and demands. But most mothers don't get fed up and throw their babies out. No, they love the child more than their own life.

And it doesn't matter what our mother was like. She could have been an angel or a devil—she still gave birth to us. She bore us for nine months in her own body, with all the discomfort and the morning sickness, and then the pain of birth. She suffered so much for us. If she had aborted us then we wouldn't be here now. She suffered so much for us and gave us the greatest gift she could have ever given us—life. And that debt of gratitude can never really be repaid.

From a Buddhist point of view, many of our endless lifetimes—most of which we do not remember—were not human. We might, for example, have been a spider and have had a mother who had hundreds of little children but nonetheless took care of them. Some species might kill the male, but they don't kill their babies. One time I saw a scorpion carrying dozens and dozens of tiny scorpions. There they were, all riding on mommy's back. We might not think of scorpions as being loving mothers, but there you are.

Gratitude for the mother is the symbol and example of the extreme gratitude that we owe to other beings. Of course, in every lifetime there are many beings that we feel gratitude toward. For example, farmers who grow all the food we consume or all the people who make the myriad things we use, we could just go on and on forever, because we are all so dependent and interconnected with other beings.

Therefore we have a debt of gratitude to repay. The greatest, most final way of repaying that debt is to attain enlightenment in order to be able to liberate others—all our mothers from endless lifetimes. According to this aspiration, we are not just practicing to make ourselves feel better. We are practicing so that in this lifetime or in future lifetimes we may be in the position to genuinely help beings, who are so desperately in need of help, whether they realize it or not. That's the motivation.

What finer gift can one offer to repay the kindness of beings than to aid them in their liberation? Right now we can aspire to do so, but we can't actually do much. It is like an armless mother watching her child being swept away by the river. We are helpless. We can't even help ourselves much less other sentient beings. But the aspiration is there. We may not be able to help effectively now, but we will from this point onward use our time to really create the causes and conditions that in the future will enable us to genuinely help in a deep and meaningful way.

After taking refuge, to enter the Mahayana path that emphasizes compassion, the path of a bodhisattva, one receives the bodhisattva vow, which is the vow to strive spiritually, not just for one's own liberation but to attain enlightenment so that in time all beings will be benefited. This doesn't mean just humans but also animals and insects, all the creatures living in the seas and the lakes, all the birds, and all the beings in the spirit realms, hell realms, and heaven realms.

Ultimately, as noted in the discussion on karma in verse 8, there are no sentient beings to be liberated and no one to liberate them anyway. The belief in an autonomous being is what prevents our liberation in the first place. But nonetheless, on a relative or conventional level, which is where we are living, this aspiration completely transforms one's own motivation: I am not doing this for me but for all beings. Also when we do something virtuous and dedicate the merit, we are doing it on behalf of other beings because they do not know how to do this. We are their representative. We perform the action, and then we dedicate the merit for all beings, so that they may rise as we rise. It is like putting yeast in the heavy dough of life, so that everything rises, not just the yeast.

The verse says, "If all the mothers who have loved me since beginningless time are suffering, what is the use of my own happiness?"

How can I be happy escaping from the burning house, if my mother is still burning? My own liberation doesn't make sense unless it is a direct cause of the liberation of all beings. To set our mind on enlightenment with the aim of liberating limitless sentient beings is the practice of a bodhisattva, because only enlightenment will give us the power, the wisdom, and the compassion to liberate all beings. Nothing else will do. This aim is the focus of the first verse of Langri Thangpa's revered *Eight Verses for Training the Mind*:

> Wishing to attain enlightenment
> For the sake of all sentient beings,
> Which excels even the Wish-Fulfilling Jewel,
> May I constantly cherish them all.[23]

The "Wish-Fulfilling Jewel" is a feature of Indian mythic tradition. It is considered to be a jewel owned by the gods that grants whatever worldly desire we may have. If we want ice cream, there is ice cream. If we want gold or diamonds, they instantly appear. A nice bright red Ferrari? Here it is! This jewel can bestow anything in the world, but it cannot give us spiritual gifts. It cannot give us insight. It cannot give us enlightenment. It can only grant mundane benefits. Our wishing to attain enlightenment for the sake of all sentient beings makes our sacred aspiration something far more rare and precious.

Remember, this means all living beings. This cannot be emphasized enough. Any beings—that live in the waters or on the earth or in the sky, throughout the universe, in all realms. These are all sentient beings. We are aspiring to attain awakening in order to help enlighten and liberate all sentient beings because, like us, all beings are trapped in the prison-house of samsara. If we can find the way to escape, we cannot just leave by ourselves; we have to open the door and help shepherd everyone else out too. This is the aspiration.

This means that all these sentient beings we have to deal with are not obstacles to our enlightenment, they are wish-fulfilling gems who help us cultivate our loving-kindness, our compassion, our patient endurance, our generosity, and all the qualities of the heart. How could we do this if we didn't have people to practice on?

We can sit in solitude and wish, "May all beings be well and happy!" Then somebody comes by and makes a noise, and we shout, "Shhh. Be quiet! I'm doing my loving-kindness meditation!" To help us avoid that kind of hypocrisy, we need other beings. We need other people to mirror us because only by relying on other sentient beings to awaken compassion and loving-kindness can we cultivate all the stages on the path. Sentient beings are precious. Therefore *may I constantly cherish them all.* May I constantly hold them dear.

In this verse, Thogme Sangpo established the aim, so what are we going to be doing for the rest of this text? Now we're going to get enlightened! And the only way to get enlightened is to make use of everything that happens to us—especially the adversities that befall us—by transforming and taking them on the path. We have to take whatever comes to us as it comes and make use of it. Then we advance.

If we only practice when all the outer conditions seem nice but not when people are noisy, or when there are problems, or when we are feeling ill, or something adverse comes up, then we don't know how to practice. We have to learn how to use our life—everything in our life—as our practice. That's it. To remind us, we have verse 11.

11

Practicing Kindness and Compassion

All suffering without exception arises from desiring
*   happiness for oneself,*
While perfect Buddhahood is born from the thought
*   of benefiting others.*
Therefore, to really exchange
My own happiness for the suffering of others is the
*   practice of a bodhisattva.*

THE REASON WHY WE SUFFER is because we are in the grip of our egoistic delusion, and we imagine that as long as we serve our own interests and can fulfill all our wants and desires, then somehow we will be happy. Other people can take care of their own happiness; it is not our concern. Our concern is to make ourselves happy. But it doesn't work. It really does not work.

The most unhappy, desperate people are those who are only thinking about their own happiness. We get caught more and more because our desires grow and grow and are endless. We are never going to be satisfied anyway. When one desire is satisfied, another desire takes its place. It is not like we can fulfill our desires and end desire for good. More desires come up, then more and more. It is endless. Our desires spiral around and around until we just end up desperate and farther and farther away from liberation. The ego just gets so bloated that in the end we are slaves to our own desires and our own grasping at material satisfaction and power. A lot of seemingly successful people end up paranoid and on alcohol or drugs of various kinds.

So the point is that if we are only thinking about our own happiness, our own satisfaction and well-being, we end up completely trapped and desperate. People put so much misdirected energy into being happy, yet they're not happy at all.

Our society presents happiness as the result of acquiring more possessions, gaining higher status, staying forever young and beautiful, being desirable to others, and along with it, defending our own territory. These are just the familiar five poisons: greed, aggression, pride, jealousy, and envy—all of which make up our ignorance or fundamental ego delusion, which Buddha himself said is the cause of suffering.

Yet our modern society projects these emotional afflictions—the very causes of suffering—as the causes of happiness. No wonder everyone is racing after satisfaction like a mirage in the desert. What looks like water and palm trees is all an illusion, and we die of thirst. It is sad that so many people are desperately chasing after a mirage.

This is why Thogme Sangpo says, "All suffering without exception arises from desiring happiness for oneself." While perfect Buddhahood, which is genuine happiness, is "born from the thought of benefiting others." If we think about others and their happiness, and we stop worrying so much about our own happiness, suddenly we find we are happy. Therefore, "to exchange my happiness for the suffering of others is the practice of a bodhisattva." This is describing the well-known practice of tonglen. In the Tibetan tradition, coming from the lojong (mind training) lineage of Atisha, tonglen is the important practice of "giving and receiving." In *Eight Verses for Training the Mind*, Langri Thangpa also advocates this practice:

In brief, directly or indirectly,
May I give all help and joy to my mothers,
And may I take all their harm and pain
Secretly upon myself.[24]

"All help and joy to my mothers"! By now this idea should be familiar to us as we discussed it at length in verse 10. Because we have been cycling endlessly through samsara since beginningless time, at some point all sentient beings have been our mother. In Asia people love and appreciate their mother, even if their mother was not especially nice. The mother was given as the example of the one person that we really wish would be free from suffering and be well and happy. We can extend that feeling of warmth and caring to all sentient beings because at some point or other we were in that same intimate relationship with them. That is the idea.

When Langri Thangpa says "directly," he means that if we are with somebody who needs help, we help them right then and there. We help them ourselves, directly. "Indirectly" means that if we are not actually in their presence, which is true of most sentient beings, we can nonetheless do meditations focused on wishing them well and happy—meditations on loving-kindness and on compassion. In that way we send out good wishes to all beings so they are indirectly affected by our wish for their well-being.

This more deliberate and focused practice of tonglen has many different applications, but in general it is based on love and compassion. Here is the basic practice: imagine someone who is suffering in any way. They could be actually present, or we can just think about them or use a photo. On the incoming breath, visualize drawing in dark light, rather like a vacuum cleaner sucking up all their suffering, including the causes of their suffering—present and karmic. Visualize drawing in their suffering in the form of black light or smoke and pollution. This goes down into the heart (the center of the chest, not the physical heart) and forms into a little black pearl that represents the self-cherishing mind; the egotistic mind doesn't want other people's suffering however sorry we may feel for them. This is the mind thinking, *Well I'm really sorry you're sick, but I'm glad it is not me!* Or *This is a very good practice, but I hope it doesn't really work.* Although we are sorry for the other's suffering, we don't want to take it on ourselves.

Visualize this dark light of others' suffering coming into ourselves and dissolving into that little black pearl of "I-ness" (because the last thing *I* want is somebody else's problems), deliberately inviting the suffering with the wish "I will take it in on myself," which crushes our self-cherishing attitude. Then as the dark light transforms into the pearl, the pearl itself transforms into a diamond and shines brightly, representing our true Buddha-nature, the pristine nature of the mind, which can never be polluted by suffering. It is eternally blissful and healthy. It cannot be anything else. It is the unconditioned and that is never polluted by the conditioned.

Our true nature is endless well-being, so as soon as the small black pearl of self-cherishing disappears, we discover our true nature, which has no problems. Then we breathe out clear white light representing all our boundless wisdom, compassion, good health, good karma—everything good within us. This light is sent out with the breath, and we visualize it melting into the person, present or imagined. Visualize every cell of their body soaked in light and being healed, so that they are completely happy and at ease. With the in-breath, we take in the darkness; with the out-breath, we give out all our bright healing qualities as clear light.

This practice can be used in many ways. For instance, if we are sick, instead of lying down and feeling sorry for ourselves, we can imagine that the suffering of all those with that particular sickness is being absorbed into us. For example, if we have a headache, then we can visualize that the headaches of all the beings in the world are drawn into us. We will take on all this sickness and free other beings from it. Or even if we are feeling sad, we can also do tonglen for ourselves. It is very beneficial. Many lamas when they are ill or dying claim that they are practicing guru yoga and tonglen.

This practice makes sense of our own suffering, and it is of great benefit to others. Many people who go to visit patients in hospitals don't know what to do when sitting with somebody who is sick or even dying. We could just hold the patient's hand and sit there doing tonglen quietly. Sometimes people coming into the room remark on the peaceful atmosphere. Or the patient says that for whatever reason they feel comforted. For instance, if we visit somebody who is sick, we can just sit there quietly doing this meditation, bringing in the dark, sending out the light. But secretly. We don't have to tell the people, "I'm doing this for you." They don't have to know that is what we are thinking or doing.

If we are in a hospital room, we don't have to sit in a special posture. We just sit. Nobody knows what we are doing. We don't need to draw attention to our practices. Even on a bus or a train or a plane, we can do tonglen. We can just take in all the problems, anxieties, and suffering of these people sitting there and give out light and love. Every single person has problems, to be sure. If it is not one thing, then it is something else. If it is not their own problems, then they are worrying about somebody close to them. Just imagine taking that all in. How wonderful if we could take in all their suffering and give them joy and happiness and well-being. I'm sure any of us would be happy to do that. If we could take everybody's suffering into ourselves and give them all joy, that would be a fair bargain since they are giving us the precious opportunity to practice compassion.

Rather than just feeling helpless in the face of suffering—apart from anything material we can do to help—inwardly, we can do these spiritual practices. If we can practice sincerely, it really does change the atmosphere. Often people just feel that something has changed. They don't know what's happened, but they feel better inside themselves. Our thoughts have tremendous power. This is important to remember.

I lived for many years in the hills behind the pilgrimage town of Assisi, where St. Francis came from. Nowadays it is all nicely smartened up and is an important pilgrimage place. Tourists who go to Italy usually visit Rome, Florence, Assisi, and Venice, so the town is full of shops selling tourist junk. Nonetheless, because it was the home of St. Francis and St. Clare, and for centuries people have visited on pilgrimage, it still has a powerful feeling. There are many beautiful medieval towns in Umbria and Tuscany, but Assisi is something special, even now, despite all the commercialism. I've met a number of people who have told me that when they went to Assisi on the tourist route, suddenly they had, out of the blue, a deep spiritual experience. They weren't expecting that at all. They weren't into any particular religious trip; they were just backpacking through Europe. But in Assisi they found that something had suddenly shifted inside them, and they had a life-changing experience there.

The town of Bodh Gaya, which sits in the midst of urban chaos, has a similar effect on people. Bihar is the most troublesome state in India. On one level it is almost a hell realm, and certainly a hungry ghost realm with all the incredible poverty and violence. Beggars, touts, and ear-splitting *bhajans* scream from the nearby temples distorted by the blaring loudspeaker systems. In the middle of this chaos sits Bodh Gaya, with a modest stone wall around it. Yet as you enter through the gate it is like being in a pure realm, especially in the early morning or evening when all the tourists have gone. It is an extraordinary place that has so much peaceful energy because of the thoughts and aspirations of all the devoted pilgrims gathered from all over the world, praying and prostrating. And of course the Buddha himself attained enlightenment there.

Similarly, if we go to Auschwitz or any of these kinds of places where something awful happened, there is actually nothing much there. It is just buildings and photos of the people who were interned and died there. But nothing more. And yet, we just know that tragedy occurred in this place. The atmosphere is so dark and heavy. The feeling of fear, suffering, and grief are still palpable because of all the awful things that happened, and the pain of all the people who have visited there since. We can feel that something horrible happened there.

The outer form of a place might not be anything threatening or anything special, but the mind force can be felt there. Whether the energy is something positive, full of love and devotion, or something negative like fear and hatred, it lingers there. We should be careful with our thoughts.

When in a situation where there is a lot of fear and paranoia, where there is anger and hatred, please do not connect with that dark energy. In the face of anger and fear, give out loving-kindness and compassion. We don't need to plug into and increase the paranoia. It doesn't help. Becoming fearful and paranoid is just increasing the problem. What we all really need to do is to replace that negative energy with positive energy. Send out loving-kindness. Cover the whole country, the whole globe with golden light of love and healing, not more and more dark energy. Please. Our thoughts have power. So make it a light positive power, not a dark negative one. Practice fearless compassion.

Our thoughts have great power, and tonglen is a practice that is motivated totally on compassion. Its genuine result not only benefits the person who is the object of the practice, but it also helps to highlight and reduce our own egotistic self-concern. This quality of selfless love that we develop really opens our heart to the suffering of the world and allows us to breathe it in and give out all the goodness within ourselves to other beings without any reservations. This is our challenge. It is both a foundational challenge and a challenge leading to the ultimate achievement: realization or awakening. Dilgo Khyentse Rinpoche explains:

> Some people may have the idea that these teachings on compassion and exchanging self and others are part of the

"gradual path" teachings of the sutras, and are not nearly as effective as the more advanced "direct path" teachings of the Great Perfection or the Great Seal. That is a complete misunderstanding. Only if you have developed the love and compassion of relative Bodhicitta can absolute Bodhicitta—the very essence of the Great Perfection and the Great Seal—ever take birth in your being.[25]

In other words, the practice of compassion is essential to the successful practice of Mahamudra or Dzogchen. Below is the tonglen practice in essence. May it be of benefit to you and all other sentient beings.

Visualize someone who is suffering

With the in-breath imagine taking in all their suffering and the causes of their suffering in the form of dark light or polluted smoke.

This dark light descends with the inhalation to the heart chakra at the center of the chest. It takes shape as a small black pearl (symbolizing the self-cherishing mind).

The black pearl immediately dissolves and is transformed into a brilliant diamond (symbolizing our Buddha-nature).

On the out-breath imagine that this diamond radiates a bright light that goes out and dissolves into the person being visualized, filling every cell of their body and mind with the clear bright light of health and happiness.

12

Embracing Adversity

If someone driven by great desire
Seizes all my wealth, or induces others to do so,
To dedicate to him [or her] my body, possessions,
And past, present, and future merit is the practice
  of a bodhisattva.

IN VERSE 12, the text follows through with a discussion of adversity. When cruel things happen to us, especially when we don't think we deserve them, how should we respond in order to carry this adversity onto the path? Tibetan Buddhism emphasizes taking everything onto the path and not discarding anything, even those things we see as big obstacles and problems, which make us think, *I would be a much better practitioner if only . . .*

Everything has to be used. It is like vegetable peelings. Instead of just discarding them as useless, we can mulch them and make them into compost that helps all the flowers and vegetables to grow even better. Likewise, rather than discarding the obstacles and problems in our lives, we can make use of them in our practice because the understanding is that if things always go too smoothly, we can be lulled into thinking that we are much more advanced practitioners than we actually are. If everyone is lovable, it is easy to be loving. Of course we want people to be friendly and kind to us, but the problem is that if we are only meeting with kindness and friendliness, it can make us think that we have no problems inside—*I'm always so kind and friendly.* This can give us a false idea that we have overcome anger, that we have overcome jealousy, that we have overcome feeling hurt, but this might not be true. Often these afflictive emotions are lying latent inside us still, only to come surging right back up when we meet with adverse people or circumstances.

However, instead of feeling upset either at the person causing this negative reaction, or at ourselves for feeling angry, we think, *Oh good, this person is so obnoxious. What a wonderful opportunity! Now I can really practice. Thank you so much for showing me how much work I still have to do. You really are my teacher. I didn't notice how sensitive I was about that and you have shown me. I'm really very grateful to you for that.*

So instead of regarding somebody who is annoying or hurtful as being the enemy, as being somebody antagonistic to us, and then getting all upset and angry, we might recognize that actually this has given us a great opportunity. It helps us to see ourselves much more clearly—what work needs to be done still and at the same time the opportunity to get to work on the remedy.

Just changing our attitude can change everything. We can regard situations that once seemed so difficult as being a great spiritual opportunity for us to develop and learn. Again, it is like going to a gymnasium and being faced with a machine that is challenging and designed to test our muscles. We don't resent that machine; rather, we are grateful to it for showing that we need to do a lot more work. We don't start kicking the machine and getting all upset because it is difficult. We think, *Wow, this is giving me a really good workout,* and we come out covered in sweat and feeling fantastic. This practice of lojong is a workout in the spiritual realm that really challenges us, but the resulting inner strength is truly profound.

When we come across people who create difficulties for us or who shame us, there is this sense of *me* that comes across quite strongly: *They are insulting* me, *humiliating* me, *cheating* me. That sense of *me* that is so strong at those times can be helpful, because we see clearly what we are dealing with. If there were no *me*, there then where would the problem be? There wouldn't be any problem. Dilgo Khyentse Rinpoche lucidly points out:

> To practice in such a way also helps to eradicate your belief in a truly existing self. For, finally, your true enemies are not some ruthless people in power, some fierce raiders or merciless competitors who constantly harass you, take everything you have, or threaten you with legal proceedings. Your real enemy is your belief in a self.
>
> That idea of an enduring self has kept you wandering helplessly in the lower realms of samsara for countless past lifetimes. It is the very thing that now prevents you from liberating yourself and others from conditioned existence. If you could simply let go of that one thought of "I," you would find it easy to be free, and to free others, too. If you overcome the belief in a truly existing self today, you will be liberated today. If you overcome it tomorrow, you will be enlightened tomorrow. But if you never overcome it, you will never gain liberation.[26]

When we come into opposition with people who are humiliating or criticizing us, especially if their criticisms are not even true, then that sense of defensiveness becomes clear. Since this is what we are dealing with, we feel grateful for their help. This is exactly the central part of this text—how to take these challenging situations involving the eight worldly concerns—praise and blame, gain and loss, pleasure and pain, and fame and infamy—onto the path and use them for our spiritual progress toward inner transformation. This is the heart of the matter in many of the verses, and each verse is dealing with a slightly different nuance of problems that arise in our daily life.

Normally, when someone steals things from us, we get upset, feel deprived, and, of course, we want to get our things back again.

This verse is not saying that, for example, if someone steals our passport, credit cards, and so on, we shouldn't go to the police to try and get them back. But from the point of view of practice, suppose for example, we have wealth, and someone robs us. There are two issues here: first, if we are robbed, it is the result of having stolen from someone else in the past—some past karmic action we had ourselves performed. Now that karmic debt is cleared up, so that is nice. Second, if someone takes everything we own, then we no longer have to protect it. The more people have, the more they need alarm systems and guard dogs and triple locks and surveillance systems. The wealthier we get, the more incarcerated we are by our possessions. If we don't have much, then it is highly unlikely that anyone is going to bother to take it, and if we do lose it, so what? Instead of getting all upset if people steal things from us, we can say, "In this and future lives, I will offer all my body, possessions, and merit." We don't even get caught up in creating a nice merit bank account for the future. We offer everything—take it all, you are welcome.

The idea of cherishing even those who are committing misdeeds is the focus of the fourth verse of Langri Thangpa's *Eight Verses for Training the Mind*:

> When I see ill-natured people,
> Overwhelmed by wrong deeds and pain,
> May I cherish them as something rare,
> As though I had found a treasure trove.[27]

This is the essence of the lojong approach: to take situations that are normally regarded as obstacles and transform them into spiritual opportunities. This is not some New Age jargon. This is genuine Buddha Dharma. I remember one time going to visit a traditional Tibetan lama who had never been to the West. I was complaining to him about all the problems I was having, and he said exactly this: "If you say it's an 'obstacle,' it's an obstacle. If you say it's an opportunity, it's an opportunity." It all depends on how we take it.

We need to develop compassion, loving-kindness, patience, and generosity with the behavior of others. We need to cultivate an open, flexible heart-mind. How can we learn these qualities if everyone only does and says everything we want them to say and do? Then we may think, *I'm such a kind, friendly person. Everybody loves me and I love everybody.* But if we only love everybody because everybody loves us, we don't learn anything. The reason why the celestial deva realms are regarded as a spiritual dead end is because everything there is too lovely. We have beautiful bodies of light, we have wish-fulfilling trees and wish-granting gems. Anything we want we get. It is all love and peace.

Sometimes when everything goes smoothly and beautifully, people don't have much incentive to practice. Why bother to practice when I'm having such a great time? In the celestial realms everybody is beautiful and never ages. As long as the good karma that caused that rebirth lasts, it is all lovely. But everything is impermanent, and even the celestial realms are still within the wheel of samsara. And since we have not been making any interest on that merit, when the balance in that merit bank begins to decline and runs out, then we have to leave the celestial realms and be reborn again. Meanwhile we haven't learned anything.

To encourage us on the path there is the carrot and the stick. The carrot is the assurance that with practice we will feel better, more calm and clear, and we will feel more at ease within ourselves. We will genuinely be able to be of more benefit to other sentient beings and so forth. The stick, or whip, is the difficulty in our daily life. These are the things that drive us on to develop a wholly different relationship with adverse circumstances and difficult people, which is what is going to help us to cultivate compassion and patient endurance and kindness and generosity.

Therefore, whenever we see "ill-natured people overwhelmed by their strong misdeeds and sufferings," we need to "treasure them as something rare." These are the people who are going to help with our practice. People who are difficult, people who challenge us in any way are the people who are going to help us on the spiritual path. Rather than avoid them, we are grateful for them, for their support in helping us to cultivate these qualities. How are we going to learn otherwise? If we don't exercise we are never going to get strong muscles. Inside we are going to be spiritually flabby. We can manage when everything is nice and pleasant, and the road is smooth and beautifully paved. But the minute it gets a bit bumpy, with ruts and potholes, then we can't drive. We just stall. This is the most important point.

There is a story of a Zen monk who was quite poor and lived in a hermitage. One day he came back to find that his hut had been broken into and everything had been taken from him—his pots and pans, stores of food, everything. He looked around and then went outside where it was nighttime and the moon was full. He looked at the sky and said, "Oh, I wish I could have given him the moon!" It is a feeling that whatever the thieves took, we want them to take more, we want them to be happy. If they stole, it is because they have negative emotions in their minds or maybe they have a great need. If they took money then we can think, *I hope he really needs that money; maybe he needs to educate or feed his children. Hopefully he doesn't just use it on drink and puts it to some good use. I'm happy for him.* If the money's gone anyway, why worry? Whether or not the money is returned, the point is either we feel upset, angry, and deprived, or we say to ourselves, *Oh well, that's cleared up that karma, and I hope that now he's content because he made a really good haul. Good that I made one sentient being happy today!*

It is usually not the situation itself that causes the problem. It is our reaction to it that causes the problem. When we create the suffering for ourselves, it is not the perpetrator who is suffering. We have the suffering of loss, and we have the suffering of resentment, so we have double suffering. This doesn't mean we don't lock our doors and take sensible precautions, but it does mean that when we lose things then we accept we have lost them, but really, so what? When things happen in life that I don't want to happen, I usually say to myself, *If this was the worst thing that was happening in the world at this moment, this would be a pure land.* Because really most of our problems are so irrelevant compared to the dreadful things that are happening to other people right now, so why do we get so upset? More on this topic follows in verse 13.

13

Bringing Suffering
onto the Path

If, in return for not the slightest wrong of mine,
Someone were to cut off even my very head,
Through the power of compassion to take all his
    negative actions
Upon myself is the practice of a bodhisattva.

THIS IS RELEVANT at this time because in many countries gov-
erned by totalitarian regimes, including Tibet, many people are
hauled off to prisons and savagely tortured or executed through no
wrongdoing of their own. Again, this is something that is not just
theory but is actually happening all around the world.

Tibet is a good example. So many great lamas and others were
imprisoned and cruelly treated, interrogated, and tortured for twenty
to twenty-five years. They hadn't done anything wrong as far as this
lifetime was concerned. Many of them were great masters. They
probably recited to themselves this exact text, which they would
have learned when they were young monks, because when they were
released after years of imprisonment in labor camps, instead of being
bitter and angry and feeling they had just wasted their lives, they
came out radiant—thin but shining, with their eyes just glowing.

As is well known, His Holiness the Dalai Lama asked one of
these political prisoners what had been his greatest fear, and the
former prisoner said, "My greatest fear was losing compassion for

my tormentors." Clearly he didn't lose compassion, because he just radiated that love. We also hear these real practitioners say how grateful they were for undergoing these hardships. Otherwise all of this stuff is just theory, precepts that we can learn by heart. But when we are faced with someone whose only thought is to harm us—even though we have never done anything to hurt them in this lifetime—how are we going to respond? Well, either we can react with anger, fear, hatred, and fantasies of retaliation, or we can think, *This poor person is acting like this because of their own delusions. How sad! I take all their negativity onto myself, and I give them all of my virtue and merits. May they have great happiness, may they find peace!* And the more difficult it gets, the more we extend to them compassion and loving-kindness. It can be done. Either we go under—and end up bitter, revengeful, and full of self-pity—or we surmount and take everything that happens to us as a teaching on the path.

Although few of us are going to be imprisoned, beaten, and interrogated, there are always situations happening in life, such as people who don't act the way they should for no ostensible reason. Why should they be so nasty? How do we act or react to them? Do we take it as an opportunity for enhancing our practice and benefiting them through our thoughts of loving-kindness—or not? Do we act like ordinary people who have never heard a word of Dharma? Sometimes I remind our nuns that it is not having a shaved head and wearing robes that make us a Dharma practitioner; it is how we respond to everyday circumstances. If someone does something we don't want them to or speaks to us rudely or criticizes us, how do we respond?

When an Australian friend of ours drives on Indian roads, which are a great challenge (especially when someone cuts you off on a blind curve or stops dead with no indication), she comes out with quite ripe language to express her feelings and then immediately adds, "And may you be well and happy!" So as long as we remember that bit . . .

In the case where we haven't done anything wrong and others are being mean, the other point to consider is that we ourselves created the causes from past lives. Nothing just happens without a cause either in this life or in some past life; these seeds were planted and they are now coming up. If we respond with anger, indignation, or fear, we are just creating more negative karma, whereas if we respond with patience and love and understanding then that karma becomes purified completely.

Sometimes I get letters from people who reiterate how they got cheated out of some property or someone abused them maybe even thirty years ago. It is so sad. I keep reminding them that all this happened in the past. Just let it go and consider right *now* what have you got? They are creating their own suffering, far more than the person who cheated them. It is like having a wound that if we leave alone will start to heal itself, but if we keep scratching then it just gets worse and, in the end, becomes infected and poisons our whole system.

We cannot base our lives on anger, resentment, and fear. His Holiness the Dalai Lama is a wonderful example of how to cope skillfully with unfair oppression, as is Aung San Suu Kyi, who has been under so much pressure and faced so many difficulties and no doubt a lot of fear under that repressive government. But still while under house arrest, instead of using her time to write scathing letters around the world about the awful government, she meditated, read books, thought constructively, and tried to use that time to inwardly develop as a bodhisattva.

If we are faced with someone who is especially difficult, we can try to just put ourselves in their shoes. How would we like to have their mind? What would it be like? Then we feel natural compassion because people don't harm others unless they themselves are hurting inside. A person who is completely happy and at peace with themselves doesn't need to hurt others. In the end it all comes back to our own inner response—not what happens to us but how we deal with what happens to us, skillfully or unskillfully. Dilgo Khyentse Rinpoche taught that "in return for harm, a bodhisattva tries to give help and benefit."[28] This brings us to verse 14.

14

Not Retaliating When We Are Harmed

Even if someone says all sorts of derogatory things about me
And proclaims them throughout the universe,
In return, out of loving-kindness,
To extol that person's qualities is the practice of a bodhisattva.

NOW IT IS COMMON that if someone says something unkind about us then we will want to say something nasty about them. Then they say something even meaner, and we respond predictably and nothing is resolved. This just creates a lot of bad feelings, anger, and aggression, and obviously this is not the way to behave.

If someone says something critical about us, then the first thing to consider is whether or not it is true. Are they pointing out some hidden fault that we hadn't noticed? If so, we can be grateful. Or, if it is totally untrue, so what? If it is not true, one doesn't need to keep defending oneself because the gossip will eventually disappear like dark clouds in the sky. However, if, for example, we are running a Dharma center and are accused of falsifying the accounts or some such and this is not true, then it is fair enough that we should try to prove our integrity. Otherwise these false rumors could harm the Dharma center and bring suspicions against others also. But we should do this without defensiveness or aggression and certainly without pointing an accusing finger at the other person. In fact, far from retaliating, we are advised, out of kindness, to extol that person's qualities.

So when someone says something unkind about us, instead of returning the favor we can say everything we can think of that is truly good about that person. We are not just pretending and over-inflating so that everyone knows really we are just gritting our teeth. But genuinely, out of loving-kindness, from our good heart, we can appreciate that person's good qualities. Then instead of ending up in a battle, we can end the conflict by neutralizing it. If we have drunk poison, we don't administer another poison; we use an antidote. The antidote to criticism is praise; responding with praise might also undermine their negativity because they are not expecting us to turn around and say nice things about them. It may well be that when they hear these good sounds, they will start to change their opinion also.

Prior to speaking nicely about that person we can cultivate our good thoughts about them, speaking from a mind of loving-kindness. We can say to ourselves, *Although they might be difficult, still from my side I did not retaliate, I really tried to take that challenge on the path. I honestly aimed to think good things about that person since we all have good qualities as well as difficult ones, and I tried to think and act as a genuine Dharma person should.*

Everything comes from cultivating the right attitude in the first place. It is not just that we are pretending to be bodhi-sattvas. The essence of our practice is to learn how to overcome our self-cherishing attitude. Therefore, in all these unpleasant situations what is hurt? It is that sense of I have been harmed. I have been humiliated. I want to have a good reputation. I want people to say nice things about me, so then I am happy. But when somebody says mean things about me, or doesn't do what I want them to do, this creates problems for me. It is all about me.

Genuine bodhisattvas act spontaneously, without this sense of self and other. All genuine spiritual traditions try to deal with the "little self" so that it can dissolve and open up into something so much more. In Buddhism there are many ways offered for doing this—meditations on emptiness, meditations on the nature of mind, vipashyana, Mahamudra, Dzogchen, tantra—all of it helps us to see through the delusion of this seemingly solid, eternal, and unchanging me at the center: to dissolve into pure awareness so much more vast and spacious.

Lojong training is doing this from the point of view of everyday thoughts and emotions, because we can talk about emptiness, Buddha-nature, and the nature of mind, but if someone says something nasty to us, and we growl, "Well it is all empty . . . yeah, but you said . . ." we discover that we haven't yet integrated those ideas into practical application in our lives. Buddhism teaches us to practice on all levels, and this is the level that deals with everyday life, relationships, and challenging things that come up. How are we responding? Are we responding genuinely as someone sincerely wishing to integrate the Dharma into our lives or just like an ordinary person?

It is when we deal with everyday occurrences that we can see how we're responding, not when we go to Dharma centers and chant beautifully. In everyday life, when someone does something that we don't like and hurts us, how do we react? If we do become angry, upset, and humiliated, we ought not to be angry with ourselves because we are angry since that creates a spiral. Instead we should reflect on the fact that this shows us how much work we still have to do. Good, now we know; we can cultivate humility and try again. Perhaps later we can rerun that scene and try to imagine a different and more positive response. As we continue to do this, gradually new patterns of behavior grow.

When someone says something bad to little children, they get upset. If everything goes the way they want, they are happy, but when it doesn't, they get distraught and sometimes quite out of control with their emotions. That's because they are young, and they don't know how to deal with their turbulent feelings. But we are grown up now, and the sign of being truly adult and mature is that we are able to cope with our emotions and able to see what is not helpful and needs to change. This doesn't happen overnight, but gradually we can change until to our own surprise we find that even when someone does something really mean, we actually don't care. "So what? May you be well and happy!" Then we get the feeling that maybe something is shifting inside. Dilgo Khyentse Rinpoche told a great story about how the legendary master Langri Thangpa, a pure monk and master of the Kadampa tradition, dealt with gossip and slander:

> Once, in the region of the cave where he [Langri Thangpa] was meditating, there was a couple whose children always died in infancy. When yet another child was born to them, they consulted an oracle, who said that the child would survive only if they claimed that he was the son of a spiritual master. The wife took her baby boy up to Langri Thangpa's cave, and set him down in front of the sage. She said, "Here is your son," and went away. The hermit said nothing about it apart from simply asking a devoted woman he knew to feed and care for the child. Sure enough, since Langri Thangpa was a monk, gossip spread about him having fathered a child. A few years later, the parents of the boy came with large offerings, and respectfully said to him, "Please forgive us. Although you were not in the least at fault, we let ill rumors spread about you. The child has survived due only to your kindness." Serene as always, Langri Thangpa gave the boy back to his parents without a word.[29]

Here is the fifth verse of Langri Thangpa's *Eight Verses for Training the Mind*:

> When someone out of envy does me wrong
> By insulting me and the like,
> May I accept defeat
> And offer the victory to them.[30]

When people say bad things about us, they are nasty, and they use harsh language and criticize us, what are we supposed to do? Normally, when we are in opposition to others, our main objective is to crush them and be victorious. Here, we are turning the whole situation around and thinking, "If they want to be victorious, let them win. May they be happy. I will take the defeat. That's all right. It doesn't harm me. If they want it, they can have it."

A friend of mine in Australia had a wealthy father. When the father died, there was a dispute between my friend and her brother about the will. Although the property and the money had all been divided half and half, her brother said that she shouldn't have anything because she wasn't living where the father had been, was not in regular contact, and therefore, the brother should have it all. He wanted to take his sister to court about this and contest the will.

She herself lived modestly, although she is an extremely talented woman, but her brother was a wealthy businessman, so she thought, *Honestly, do I want to go to court? He is very wealthy, and he is going to employ top lawyers. I can only afford the least expensive. Then I'll have to keep attending court for weeks, months, and maybe years. Not only will it cost a fortune, it will also create a lot of acrimony between us, and for what? True, I don't have much money, but so what? It is enough. If it will make my brother happy to have all this extra money when he already has so much, then, may he be well and happy!*

So she did not contest the case and allowed him to take all the money. She just went on with her life, and she's still going on with her life. I don't know what the brother is doing. One doubts if he is any happier for having a few million more. But she was free because she remembered this verse: "May I take defeat on myself and offer the victory to others." She gave the victory to her brother. But in the end, she got the real victory because she was free. She didn't have all the worries and hassles of going through a bitter court case just for the sake of money. Meanwhile, her brother presumably felt self-satisfied and happy. That is nice, and it becomes a win/win situation.

Consider certain sports where there are two teams. One is sure to win, one is bound to lose. We are happy for those that win. We are miserable if the team we like loses and more miserable if we are actually on the team that loses. Imagine if the team that lost rejoiced in the victory of their opponents, and the victorious team also applauded the team that lost. Everybody would be happy, everybody would win. We ourselves determine what it means to win or lose. If we can just cheerfully hand over the victory to others, then we have also won. Do you understand?

This obviously does not mean that if we are in an abusive situation, we just allow the abuse to take place, or if we are faced with somebody who is trying to cheat us or do us harm, we just allow them to get away with it. Apart from the fact that we don't want to be injured, karmically it is also bad for them. In that case, what we need is a kind of fearless compassion that deals with that negative situation not with anger or fear but with a compassionate heart, recognizing that the other person is causing a lot of problems for themselves and for others and has to be stopped.

Patient endurance itself is a strength; it is not a weakness. Getting upset and angry and wanting to fight back is weak. But having the ability to stand back and look at the situation and decide from an inner poise the most skillful way to act—that is strength. So many times, the most skillful way is just to say, "All right, you win," and walk away. Lay down the burden of having to be right. There is no problem then. They are happy, you are happy. Everybody is happy. This leads us to verse 15.

15

Respecting Even Our Enemies

Even if in the midst of a large gathering
Someone exposes my hidden faults with insulting language,
To bow to him respectfully,
Regarding him as a spiritual friend, is the practice of
*   bodhisattva.*

AGAIN, HUMILIATION IS THE EMOTION we feel when someone not only says something nasty or critical to us in private but also exposes our faults on the internet and even announces them to a crowd of people. It is a sense of incredible humiliation that gives rise to tremendous anger and a desire to hit back. Consider, for instance, the abusive language that people use at political rallies . . . these are the people who are going to rule the country! They will be making great decisions that affect the whole world, yet they can't even deal with their own minds. Often they are so out of control it is frightening. Where are the bodhisattvas?

Imagine if, during a question-and-answer session following some Dharma teaching, someone stands up and insults all my views with critical language and exposes my hidden faults to everyone present. Meanwhile I am sitting comfortably on my little throne, but cast down on the floor, as it were, and beaten up. What do I do? Well I can defend myself: "Who are you to tell me anyway? How dare you challenge my authority?" or, as Thogme Sangpo sagely recommends, I can bow respectfully and regard the critic as a spiritual friend. Why? Because anyone who reveals to us our hidden faults is a great friend. If they do that with insulting language in a large gathering, they are even more our friend because it gives the ego the opportunity to get up on its high horse and go at that person with a raised sword for daring to reveal to everybody my true nature—well, my untrue nature—and my hidden faults. Because *that* is the ultimate humiliation and reveals the ego in all its radiant glory. Then it is so clear and naked. Ego exposed!

One time a friend had asked me to her house to translate a Tibetan text. Later some jewelry of hers was stolen from the room where I had stayed. Some days later she came to visit me with another friend who thought herself to be psychic, and she claimed to have had a vision that showed that I was the one who stole the jewelry. It was so interesting, and I was in such a state of shock—me?! The sense of ego was so naked. If somebody does accuse us, whether it is true or not, there is the sense of nakedness. The lamas say that sometimes through shock we can get a clear view of the nature of the mind because conceptual thinking drops away in that moment. Unfortunately, I didn't see the nature of the mind, but I saw the nature of the ego.

So should anybody get up and insult us and expose our hidden faults whether we actually have them or not, then from our heart we should be grateful. It is important to know where our faults are. We see some, but there are others we just don't see and until something happens to bring them up, we don't even know they are there. Instead of being defensive and upset, we should be grateful and, as it says, take our accusers as a spiritual friend. Dilgo Khyentse Rinpoche reminds us that, if we want to be a genuine follower of the Buddha, we should never retaliate when we are harmed. He suggests that we remember what are called the four principles of positive training, which are as follows:

If someone abuses you, do not abuse him or her in return; if someone gets angry with you, do not get angry with him or her in return; if someone exposes your hidden faults, do not expose his or hers in return; and if someone strikes you, do not strike them back.[31]

16

Showing Kindness When We Are Wronged

Even if one I've lovingly cared for like my own child
Regards me as an enemy,
To love him even more,
As a mother loves a sick child, is the practice of a
  bodhisattva.

ONE OF THE MOST PAINFUL THINGS to accept is when we have helped and done favors for other people, and they turn around and treat us like an enemy. For instance, consider parents who have done so much for their child—lovingly raised them and given them an education—and then the child reaches teenage years and turns against the parents, blaming all their problems on the parents and being totally ungrateful. At such times there is a double pain because, first, the parents are worried about what the child will do and, second, they are hurt by their child's behavior.

This situation often happens with siblings. There are so many brothers and sisters who are taking each other to court, usually over money and property disputes. Like the case I mentioned earlier where the parent died and then there was a fight over who got what. So often these siblings end up as enemies, even though when they were children perhaps they loved and took care of each other. Another example is friends who go into business together and trust each other, and then one of them embezzles funds or does something equally hurtful and damaging.

My mother owned a fish shop left to her by my late father and she used to work there, but my uncle, my father's brother, was actually doing the buying and selling of the fish. From time to time my mother would remark that business was good, yet we seemed to be making little profit. Then one day my uncle was sick, and my mother had to go to the fish market to buy the fish herself. At the market they refused to sell her any fish because they said our shop was already over £2,000 in debt! That was a huge amount of money in those days. It turned out that my uncle was an inveterate gambler and had gambled away all our money on horse races. Instead of making a nice profit, which we had actually done, we were deeply in debt. Because he was her brother-in-law, my mother had trusted him implicitly while all those years he had been cheating us and keeping us short of money. But my mother just felt sorry for him and for his wife. Eventually, he retired from the shop and had to work elsewhere to repay the debt.

Beyond that, she didn't do anything. She didn't take him to court and didn't speak badly of him. She just accepted that it was sad that he had this addiction to gambling and that he should try to get himself healed from it. She never talked about it much, and she didn't hold a grudge in her heart. She just went on with her life. Dilgo Khyentse Rinpoche suggests:

To meet someone who really hurts you is to meet a rare and precious treasure. Hold that person in high esteem, and make full use of the opportunity to eradicate your defects and make progress on the path. If you cannot yet feel love and compassion for those who treat you badly, it is a sign that your mind has not been fully transformed and that you need to keep working on it with increased application.[32]

Of course my mother didn't know anything about treating my uncle as a rare and precious treasure, but she certainly didn't carry him as a great big lump of resentment and anger in the center of her heart. She just felt sorry for him and that compassion transformed the situation.

This practice is something useful. If a child is throwing up and bad tempered because they are sick, the mother doesn't hate the child. In fact, she loves her child all the more because they are suffering.

Likewise if people treat us badly even though we have been kind to them, in a way it is because they are sick. A person who is inwardly balanced and healthy would not act like that, so obviously they have a lot of problems inside themselves and that's how they are reacting. Instead of getting upset and angry, we can treat them like a mother treats a sick child, giving them even more sympathy and understanding.

The following verse from *Eight Verses for Training the Mind* suggests that even if people who we have treated well treat us badly, our compassion should be no weaker than the compassion we feel for a person we love who needs our help:

> Even if someone whom I have helped
> And in whom I have placed my hopes
> Does great wrong by harming me,
> May I see them as an excellent spiritual friend.[33]

Even if somebody whom we trust and in the past we have helped turns against us and tries to harm us through their speech or their actions, instead of feeling upset and self-pitying or wanting to get our own revenge, we can see them as our most precious spiritual friend. Why? Because they are teaching us the most difficult of qualities: patient endurance or forbearance, which is one of the six paramitas or perfections of virtues needed on the bodhisattva path toward awakening, or Buddhahood.

We absolutely have to practice tolerance or patient endurance, and we cannot do that unless somebody or something really upsets us. When somebody we care for turns around and harms us, and this makes us feel hurt and angry, instead of wanting to get back at them or feeling full of bewildered self-pity, we can think, *Oh, thank you, you're so kind. You have acted despicably, but I'm so grateful! Without you, how could I practice this most precious quality? So really, you are like my teacher. You are mirroring to me my own shortcomings because if you say something I don't like, I get all upset and angry. The problem is not you. Here, the problem is me. I'm going to learn how to cultivate loving-kindness, compassion, and patience in the face of your abuse and your hurtful actions.*

This is not totally idealistic. Prime examples of applying this practice are the Tibetan lamas and teachers, monks and nuns I mentioned in chapter 13 who were put in prison, interrogated, and often horribly tortured even though they hadn't done anything wrong. When they were finally released from these prisons after twenty to thirty years, many of them, rather than being embittered and broken, were radiant and brimming with love and compassion. They hadn't spent their time resenting their captors, planning revenge, or even beating themselves up thinking what bad karma they had made to be in such a situation. Instead, they used those circumstances to cultivate qualities like love, compassion, patience, and tolerance, which up until then they had just been studying and debating. They were grateful to their tormentors for giving them an opportunity to practice these qualities: "Without them, how would I have learned?" they said. "They were so helpful on the path."

These are present-day, real-life examples not some kind of fantasy world. In order to take the most difficult circumstances onto the path and transform them, we need conditions in which to practice.

All of these verses are about not getting upset, not making a double wound. To harbor resentment in our hearts and regurgitate it over and over again, what does it do? It doesn't make us happy, it doesn't help or harm the other person, and it creates negative karma for us. We do to ourselves what only our worst enemies would wish for us. It is better to practice patience and tolerance and move on.

17

Respecting Those Who Disrespect Us

Even if my peers or my inferiors
Out of pride do all they can to debase me,
To respectfully consider them like my teachers
On the crown of my head is the practice of a bodhisattva.

AGAIN, THIS IS DEALING WITH the ego and feeling humiliated. If ordinary people, like our friends or those who serve or work for us in some way—employees, taxi drivers, garbage collectors, waiters, and so on—create problems for us and say bad things about us, then instead of trying to put them down in return, we raise them up. Why? Because they are showing us our own pride, arrogance, and narrow-mindedness and how much we resent other people treating us in a way that we don't want to be treated.

Dilgo Khyentse Rinpoche put it this way:

See and respect such people as kind teachers showing you the path to liberation. Pray that you may be able to do as much good as possible for them. Whatever happens, do not wish for a moment to take your revenge. The capacity to patiently bear scorn and injury from those who lack your education, strength, and skill is particularly admirable. To remain humble while patiently bearing insults is a very effective way of countering your ingrained tendency to be interested only in your own happiness and pleasure.[34]

Often we have an attitude that makes us want people to admire us and treat us nicely. When people treat us well, we are all smiles and friendly. However, when people criticize us or don't give us the respect we think we deserve, then we get upset and think it is their fault. But again, rather than being upset and miserable, we can feel gratitude and consider how lucky we are because without adversaries how could we travel on the bodhisattva path? We can think, *Thank you. Obviously my good karma brought you along so I can get better and better. This is wonderful! I am so grateful to you for being so difficult, but at the same time I have compassion because your attitude is so horrible and I really hope that from now on you will be well and happy!*—and mean it.

It is also helpful to maintain a sense of humor, as it greatly diffuses anger and humiliation. If we can see the funny side of things then we can laugh. The ego hates to be laughed at; it takes itself very seriously, so it is important to practice not taking ourselves so seriously whenever the opportunity arises.

As an antidote, Langri Thangpa suggests in *Eight Verses for Training the Mind* that we adopt this approach:

Whenever I am in the company of others,
May I regard myself as inferior to all,
And from the depths of my heart
Cherish others as supreme.[35]

The Tibetan text actually says, "May I see myself as inferior to all other beings and hold other beings as higher than myself." In Tibet, on the whole, people had high self-esteem. Even quite humble people felt at ease within themselves. This was one of the reasons they were such an exemplary refugee group when they came out from Tibet to exile in India and Nepal. After having lost everything and witnessed the most horrific things, including their religion and culture destroyed, and having spent months trying to escape, on the whole they were not as traumatized as they should have been. They were still cheerful and kind and optimistic about what they were going to accomplish in the future.

One of the reasons for this was their incredibly deep faith. When the Tibetans escaped, many high lamas escaped too. The Tibetan refugees had their lamas with them along with their tremendous devotion to the Dharma. That kept them strong. But they also coped better than expected because they had an unshakable sense of well-being inside themselves. Even when external circumstances were so adverse, inwardly they were still strong.

Now this present text, *Eight Verses for Training the Mind*, was written by an important lama sitting on his high throne and was addressed to all the other abbots and esteemed monks. Thus, to say, "May I see myself as inferior," was an interesting way for these lamas to view themselves. They would naturally take their superior position for granted within their society. Therefore, to encourage them to take the lower place was good for them. The actual text says, "Whenever I am in the company of others, may I consider myself as the lowest." Here it is translated as, "May I regard myself as inferior to all." I think that this is more accurately the point.

There are several versions of a story about a meeting between His Holiness the Dalai Lama and eminent neuroscientists and psychologists during a Mind and Life conference. It seems His Holiness must have been talking about how, in the company of others, one sees oneself as most inferior. In response to that, one of these eminent psychiatrists said, "Yes, but what about low self-esteem?" His Holiness looked blank and asked his translator what the psychiatrist meant. The translator presumably tried to translate "low self-esteem" in Tibetan, for which there is no word. His Holiness thought about it and then said, "I think, very rare." The psychiatrist turned to his eminent colleagues and asked, "Who here suffers from low self-esteem and self-hatred?" They all put up their hands.

For His Holiness, that was probably a revelation because Westerners always appear like we know it all, and we go around the world telling everybody else how they should do things. We present a façade of total confidence and belief in ourselves. It is only when we take off that mask that we find underneath there is low self-esteem, inner criticism, a sense of inner failure, and so forth that is masked by this persona of total confidence.

The four Brahma-viharas (four immeasurable qualities) of loving-kindness, compassion, joy, and equanimity are traditionally practiced by sending these positive thoughts first to ourselves, then to those we feel affection for, those we feel neutral about, those we have problems with, and finally to all living beings in general. The Dalai Lama's main translator, Geshe Thupten Jinpa, when he started teaching about the Brahma-viharas in America, discovered to his surprise that Americans could not love themselves. They had tremendous resistance to giving themselves loving-kindness and compassion. He had to change it around and say, "Start with somebody you love. Start with your partner, your children, your parents, or your pet dog or cat, whoever you love. Just give them loving-kindness. Just imagine how wonderful it would be if they were happy and free from suffering. Then, when you feel that warm glow inside, turn it on yourself."

If this line is translated literally as meaning "most inferior," we might react by thinking, *Oh, look at me. I'm hopeless, I'm stupid. They're so wonderful, but not me, I'm useless.* When we already have low self-esteem that kind of interpretation would make us end up feeling more depressed and hopeless, which is not what is intended. In Buddhism, *pride* means thinking we are superior to other people, but it also means thinking we are inferior to other people. If I think, *Oh, I'm the most stupid person here, I'm hopeless, I can't do anything. All these people, they're so wonderful. When they're in retreat, they're deep in the first dhynana or at least samadhi. I'm the only one that's been caught up in all the wandering thoughts.* That is not humility. That is just the inverse of ego clinging, the dualistic mind beating itself up. The ego is happy to be miserable because if we are miserable, especially full of self-pity about how awful and hopeless and stupid we are, what are we thinking about? Me, me, me. Poor me! Oh, stupid me! Hopeless me! Me. And then we hire therapists and sit there talking about me. If our sense of self is healthy, we don't have to think about ourselves that much because we are thinking about others. We can get off our own back.

Therefore, here, if this line is translated as, "Whenever I'm in the company of others, may I consider myself least important," it more accurately conveys the point. When we meet with other people, we consider them more important and more interesting. Our attention is on the other people, making them happy. Our attention should not be on what they are thinking about us. We shouldn't be thinking, *Do they like me? Don't they like me? Do I give a good impression? Do they think I'm stupid?* Blah, blah, blah. If we are thinking like that, we are trapped in our ego, and we cannot see or deeply listen to the other person because we are too busy talking to ourselves about ourselves. The point about our attitude when we meet with others is that the other person, whoever it is, at that moment is the most important person in the world because that is the person we are with. When we have that attitude, we can get out of the way and truly see the other person. We hear them.

Essentially, that is what Langri Thangpa is saying: in the company of others, just get out of the way. That person, whoever we are with, is the most important person at that moment because they are who we are with right now. Which is why he says, "and from the depths of my heart to cherish others and hold them supreme."

In other words, all beings want to be well and happy. They don't want to suffer. We might have strange ideas about where our happiness lies, but nonetheless we would all rather feel well inside than suffer. In addition, as the Buddha said, "To each one, her own self is most dear." In other words, each individual is the center of their own universe until they awaken. One way to help dissolve that self-absorption, that total preoccupation with ourselves, is to cherish others as most dear, most important—because, just like us, they would rather be happy than miserable. Who wouldn't? In addition, there are zillions more other beings, and there is only one little me. By sheer weight of numbers other beings are more important.

People are always complaining they have no time to practice. What nonsense. We are sitting in a plane or a train or we are stuck in a traffic jam, surrounded by all these other people. Imagine sending out rays of golden light of love and compassion to all these people who are usually not looking very happy. Send them love. Just imagine that suddenly their hearts are filled with inner joy. Wouldn't that be wonderful? All these beings would love to feel joy. Wish it for them. Imagine that it is so. We don't have to sit up in our chair cross-legged, especially not while driving. Just relax and imagine. Maybe just give an intentional genuine smile from the heart. How beautiful if all these people would be well and happy, free from suffering and all their problems solved. So happy. The heart of this is simply to cherish all beings. Each being is totally important to themselves. Remembering that, we give them love and wish them well.

All these verses, by both Langri Thangpa and Thogme Sangpo are, over and over again, dealing with situations that come up in our relationships with others, causing us pain and hurt. The question is how to transform that pain and bring it into our practice and at the same time cultivate those very qualities we are trying to cultivate. It is all right to sit on our cushions and think, *May all beings be well and happy. May all beings be free from suffering.* But when those beings come right in front of us and do nasty, unkind things or say things like, "You've got just forty-eight hours to get out of the country," as was said to me in my retreat cave all those years ago, then these are the sentient beings that we want to be well and happy and free from suffering. This is the point.

This is a practical teaching on how to make use of the difficulties in life without getting upset, without getting uptight or reactive, and also without getting tense toward ourselves. Because if we are really giving out loving-kindness and compassion, these are warming emotions that also heal our own heart. While we are giving loving-kindness and compassion to others we are also giving loving-kindness to ourselves. We are sentient beings, and we are the sentient being that we are most responsible for, so we definitely need to send lots of loving-kindness and compassion to ourselves, too. In fact, if we genuinely had loving-kindness and compassion toward ourselves, we would naturally have it toward others; it would just naturally overflow. The reason we get upset and angry quickly is because inside we do not feel at peace with ourselves and, ironically, since we are always criticizing ourselves, we get defensive when others criticize us too.

We have to also work on cultivating our heart to become more open and spacious and loving and peaceful, starting from where we are right now, so that gradually goodwill can naturally begin to radiate out. Otherwise, if we are very taut like a drum, everything that touches us makes a loud noise. But if we are relaxed and soft inside like cotton wool, even if something hits us it doesn't make any noise. Inside ourselves we should feel relaxed and peaceful with a sense of humor, more at home with ourselves, so that whatever happens on the outside will not be so difficult to handle; we can deal with it.

It has to be understood that this text of Thogme's presents the summit of how a great bodhisattva naturally acts. Although we are not going to spontaneously act in the way recommended in these verses each time these events occur, we take it as a training program. When first we sit down to play the piano, we cannot right away play a Beethoven sonata. We start with scales and hit all the wrong notes. It may sound terrible, but if we keep practicing and practicing, eventually the music will flow. Likewise with our minds, when these situations come up, perhaps there will be instances in our mind where we will think, *Now pause a minute; this is my opportunity to practice.* That's why this is called *mind training.* We are training so that we don't respond unskillfully with negative reactions but instead with understanding and compassion.

This is why it is good to memorize some of the lojong texts such as the *Eight Verses for Training the Mind* and *The Thirty-Seven Verses on the Practice of a Bodhisattva.* We can quickly bring a verse to mind, and it will be a reminder of how to act as a genuine practitioner, rather than just an ordinary person. I am sure that if someone got up in the middle of a big assembly and started insulting His Holiness the Dalai Lama, he would laugh and look at him with great compassion. His Holiness wouldn't feel insulted and upset or start saying nasty things back. Of course the security guards would come, but the spontaneous response of His Holiness would be only compassion.

His Holiness often says that as a boy he had a very bad temper, so this lojong has been one of his main practices. He's obviously used all the awful things that have happened in his own country and to his beloved people to develop more and more compassion and less and less anger, retaliation, and bitterness. He must definitely see this life as a great training program, because it is relentless. Yet he never fails to be compassionate and that is why he is universally loved. We can see before us an example of how to respond skillfully in even the most difficult circumstances. It can be done.

18

Being Compassionate When Things Are Difficult

*Even when utterly destitute and constantly maligned
    by others,
Afflicted by terrible illness and prey to evil forces,
To still draw upon myself the suffering and wrongdoing
    of all beings
And not lose heart is the practice of a bodhisattva.*

SO THIS VERSE, TOO, EMPHASIZES the practice of tonglen toward someone who is suffering or who is ill or who has any problems. We visualize taking on their suffering. However, we can also practice for ourselves, if we are suffering or ill or maligned or when something difficult is happening to us or we are completely destitute. Instead of just despairing, we can practice tonglen and think of all those beings in the world who are suffering what we are experiencing right now. We can say, "May all their suffering ripen in me and may they be free of their suffering. May all my inherent good qualities, the endless potential of my Buddha-nature, along with whatever good karma I may have, may all of that be given to them. May they be free of suffering, may all their suffering ripen upon me."

In that way, surprisingly enough, we do not end up feeling totally despairing and suicidal. Actually, what happens is that we feel a kind of inner empowerment and a meaning and purpose to our suffering. We are not just thinking *poor me*. As Dilgo Khyentse Rinpoche suggests:

> Suffering, in fact, can be helpful in many ways. It spurs your motivation, and, as many teachings point out, without suffering there would be no determination to be free of samsara. Sadness is an effective antidote to arrogance.[36]

With this attitude to suffering, we find ourselves willing to be the surrogate for all the other beings in the world. We can think, *If only their suffering could come to me, how happy I would be*—just like a mother rejoicing in taking on the pain of her child. When we are caught in suffering, we can open our hearts away from our own personal woe to recognize the universality of this particular anguish.

We can also practice if we lose a loved one, by just thinking, *May the sorrow of all those in the world who have experienced the loss of a husband or a child or a parent, may all that pain come onto me. I will take their suffering. May they be free of suffering.* This may be a difficult practice, but it opens the heart when we recognize that this is a universal problem. So many people right now in this world are suffering as I am suffering, how sad. This is helpful because it prevents us from getting so caught up in our own misery that we can't admit anyone else's: *I don't care about other people's suffering, it is my suffering that counts.*

This is also a skillful way of taking suffering onto the path. Obviously if we are suffering then we try to get better, but in the meantime we can use this practice as a way of connecting with other beings who share this problem. We are not the only one, so there arises the sincere aspiration born of compassion, *Wouldn't it be wonderful if I could take on all their suffering and they would be free from that. I am happy to suffer as much as possible if others could just be free.* Then that suffering is not felt as suffering.

The Buddha said there are two types of suffering: one is the physical pain that is unavoidable with this human body. The other is the mental pain that can be avoided. One way of doing this is opening up our hearts to the pain of others instead of allowing our pain to make us more introverted, more self-pitying. This again is an important lojong practice—taking suffering on the path and using it to develop compassion and empathy. Usually when we suffer we are caught in our own dungeon of misery, and this practice opens the doors and the windows, allowing us to reach beyond ourselves.

19

Recognizing What Is Truly Valuable

Though I may be famous, and revered by many,
And as rich as the God of Wealth himself,
To see that the wealth and glory of the world are
*   without essence*
And to be free of arrogance, is the practice of
*   a bodhisattva.*

COMPARED TO THE MALIGNING and beheading in the previous verses, verse 19 will seem a little more upbeat. Generally speaking, some people are good at dealing with misfortune and taking difficulties on the path, but as soon as things start to go well, they fall apart spiritually. Others, of course, can practice nicely when things go well, but when something goes wrong, they don't know how to deal with it skillfully. Usually we are either one or the other extreme, and we need to bring balance into our lives, whether everything is going really well or problems and obstacles appear to challenge us. Either way, without hope or fear, we are learning to take whatever comes and use it as our path.

Samsara is often described as an ocean, and oceans have big waves: sometimes we are up and sometimes we are down. We need to develop inner equanimity so that whatever happens we can maintain that inner stillness and be able to cope with situations in a skillful manner without getting carried away either by grief or exaltation.

Having shown us how to deal with all the horrible things that can happen to us, Thogme Sangpo is now saying that even if things go well, if we are famous and wealthy and everybody loves us, still we should not grasp at that because we cannot take it with us. No matter how rich we may be, how many friends we have, how large our family is, or how many thousands of devotees surround us, still at the time of death we go empty-handed and alone. Dilgo Khyentse Rinpoche makes this clear:

> A Bodhisattva sees that wealth, beauty, influence, prosperity, family lineage—in fact, all the ordinary concerns of this life—are as fleeting as a flash of lightning, as ephemeral as a dew drop, as hollow as a bubble, as evanescent as the skin of a snake. He [or she] is never conceited or proud, no matter what worldly achievements and privileges may come to him [or her].[37]

We see in this day and age people who are very wealthy until they make a single mistake on the stock market and end up bankrupt. If we rely on wealth and success and popularity for our happiness, we are in a tenuous position because everything is impermanent. We see it today in the media with people who are popular world figures one minute and dragged through the mud the next. Even people like Mother Teresa and Gandhi, who have such high reputations, are only revered until somebody writes some scurrilous book about them. Many people do not like anybody to be considered superior to them, and they enjoy reading books and articles that seem to bring down revered figures and prove that everybody is as bad as everybody else. There's no need to try to improve themselves.

If we attach our sense of self and happiness purely to external values and what other people are saying about us, then we will always be insecure. It is the nature of everything to change and as Thogme Sangpo says, "The wealth and glory of this world are without essence." People can say the most fantastic things about us, whether true or untrue, and actually it doesn't alter anything—it doesn't change who we are or even make us happier. People can own a million corporate jets, but does that make them happier? It does not. It does not make them feel any better inside. Many wealthy and famous people are under a lot of pressure to maintain that glossy outer image. They are terrified that they may lose their glory and that someone will come up and be more popular. Imagine the tremendous tension those pop stars and movie stars are always under. Once you get to the pinnacle, how are you going to maintain it? Well, you are not, in fact.

If our sense of well-being and happiness depends on other people's opinions and our external possessions, that's sad, because that's not who we are at all.

Just as people saying bad things about us, whether right or wrong, should not really affect us, likewise people's praise and unrealistic projections should not change who we are. If we are dependent on the good opinions of others, then we will suffer because they are unreal, like echoes. Therefore, it is important not only to take pain and difficulties on the path but to bring good situations onto the path as well. We bring not just pain on the path but also pleasure; not just loss but also gain; not just blame, but also praise; and not just insignificance but also fame. All of it has to be taken and made use of on the path.

Usually we imagine that our problems would be solved if only we could avoid the unpleasant and gain only the pleasurable. However, these are two sides of the same coin. If we cling to one and try to avoid the other, then we are trapped in a mundane state of being that is insecure, because we are never going to get all the things we want and avoid all the things we don't want.

The point is to remain open to whatever comes, to whichever side of the coin turns up. To just stay balanced like a boat on the waves. The waves go up and the waves go down, but the boat just glides through.

One of the problems with being famous, rich, revered, or successful is that we tend to cling to those states and often become proud. Wealthy multimillionaires hang out with other multimillionaires. They don't want to deal with the hoi polloi down below. They have their private jets and their darkened windows so nobody can see them in their cars; their mansions have high walls around them with guards and dogs. That's very sad, isn't it? Imagine being like that. It is partly because they're afraid, of course; it's certainly not a sign of being happy and at peace. But apart from millionaires, even average people who are happy and comfortable with lots of friends who say nice things about them should not cling to those things, nor allow their happiness to depend only on everything being pleasant and smooth.

When I first got ordained at the age of twenty-one, I went to Thailand, and a Thai princess invited me to her estate by the ocean. I had only been ordained for a few weeks and here I was in this beautiful, polished teak house situated in the center of a lotus pond. There were three servants preparing delicious Thai food and through the mango grove was her private silver beach beside the ocean. I said to her, "I am supposed to have renounced the world and now I am living like this! I really feel guilty and quite uncomfortable with the situation." She wisely replied, "No, you didn't ask for this, you didn't seek it, but because of your good karma it has come to you. It is not going to last for long, and maybe afterward you will be poor and live in difficult conditions. When things go well, be happy, and when things are difficult, be happy also. Just keep an even mind."

Perversely, we can sometimes cling to poverty as much as we cling to wealth. I know some people who are quite ascetic in their practice, and if they are taken to a nice restaurant, they feel uncomfortable. They are only happy hanging out in the local cheap

Indian *dhabas*. The point is, if we are in a nice restaurant, that's great; if we are in a scruffy old dhaba, that's nice too—who cares? Whatever comes, just take it and enjoy, don't cling to it. Practicing equanimity of mind toward whatever comes is best. When things ride smoothly that's nice, and when the going gets bumpy that's okay too.

20

Giving Peace a Chance

If one does not conquer one's own hatred,
The more one fights outer enemies, the more they will
*   increase.*
Therefore, with the armies of loving-kindness and compassion,
To tame one's own mind is the practice of a bodhisattva.

Now Thogme has been saying that if we get angry at people who are difficult for us and retaliate, it is like pouring oil on the fire—it just burns brighter and brighter. As Buddha said, hatred never ceases through hatred; hatred ceases through nonhatred or love. The more we retaliate, the more the problems continue to increase, as we see in world politics. The aggression will persist until we agree to let go of our differences. We are all human beings sharing the same planet. At least let's try and make this a good home to live in.

Family members who are always fighting one another will be miserable no matter how beautiful the home is. On the other hand, if the family is living in a hovel but stays together in harmony and love, then there is happiness. Likewise with this beautiful planet we inhabit. If we are endlessly in conflict with each other, fueled by jealousy, greed, and aggression, then even though it could be a pure land, it remains samsara. The planet is not samsara. It is the minds of the beings that inhabit the planet that creates samsara—or Nirvana.

If we entered Nirvana, we wouldn't suddenly disappear! We would still be living on this same planet, but everything would be transformed because the mind transformed. It all depends on the mind. Everything depends on the mind. If we don't deal with our own mental defilements, then nothing will ever evolve on this planet. Even though people are becoming more aware of how we are destroying our only home, the devastation continues unchanged regardless of how many laws are passed or how many environmental groups are formed.

Why are we destroying our own planet? The reason is that the anger, greed, and delusion are now totally out of control, encouraged by our consumer society. Our education systems, the media, and our governments are controlled or at least heavily influenced by rapacious multinational corporations. The planet simply cannot sustain it all.

However, all of this originates from the uncontrolled mind, raging with greed and anger and envy and confusion. So many mental negativities! Then there is the human arrogance that thinks we can do whatever we want to other species, or that we belong to a superior race, which permits us to suppress others and seize their assets to use for ourselves. This has happened throughout history, but we never seem to learn.

Where do the wars, the capitalist corporate aggression, and greed beyond words all come from? They all come from the uncontrolled mind that dominates our speech, our thinking, and our actions. If we multiply that by seven billion we can see where the problem lies. We cannot just blame the politicians; we have to look closer. From a worldwide perspective we gradually draw in closer and closer; we might focus on Dharma centers, families, relationships between couples, and again we find greed, aggression, and ignorance. Especially the ignorance of believing our own ideas are the truth: *What I think must be right, because that is what I think.*

When Thogme Sangpo says, "If one does not conquer one's own hatred, the more one fights outer enemies, the more they will increase," he is speaking about anger. When there is anger inside our heart, we fight with one person, then another, and then we get irritated and quarrel with someone else. It goes on in an endless cycle. We can always find something to complain about, and it is always somebody else's fault. All of us know people with angry minds who regard themselves as blameless and other people as difficult and problematic. They don't see that on one or two occasions that might be true, yet a history of conflictive relationships indicates that the problem is not out there, but within themselves. How come we've ended up with so many enemies when we started out with so many friends? It follows then, the more one fights outer enemies, the more they will increase. As Dilgo Khyentse Rinpoche explains:

> Once you overcome the hatred within your own mind, you will discover that in the world outside there is no longer any such thing as even a single enemy. But if you keep giving free rein to your feelings of hatred and try to overcome your outer adversaries, you will find that however many of them you manage to defeat there will always be more to take their place. Even if you could subjugate all the beings in the universe, your anger would only grow stronger. You will never be able to deal with it properly by indulging it. Hatred itself is the true enemy, and cannot be allowed to exist. The way to master hatred is to meditate one-pointedly on patience and love. Once love and compassion take root in your being, there can be no outer adversaries.[38]

To counter this endless cycle of hatred that creates more and more enemies, Thogme Sangpo suggests we recruit loving-kindness and compassion:

> Therefore, with the armies of loving-kindness and
>   compassion,
> To tame one's own mind is the practice of a bodhisattva.[39]

To assemble these armies of loving-kindness and compassion we start by befriending ourselves. As the Buddha recommended, loving-kindness and compassion should first be sent to ourselves. A lot of our anger that is directed toward others stems from our initial anger toward ourselves. First we have to cultivate peace within ourselves, forgive ourselves, and appreciate that despite all our faults and problems, essentially we are good. We do have Buddha-nature, so there is definite hope that we can improve, and we must be friends with ourselves.

If we want to tame a wild horse, first we have to befriend that horse. Certainly we can beat it into submission and then the horse, though he hates us, will obey, like many of these poor donkeys that we see carrying too-heavy loads. But who wants a broken-down hack for a mind? A more skillful way is to befriend the wild horse, allow it to gradually calm down and recognize that it is not going to be hurt, that actually this could be a worthwhile and fun relationship. Then gradually the horse begins to quiet and slowly become more amenable. Once the horse begins to trust, then we can start to train.

All this emphasis on how to deal with others is based on the idea that we have pacified and befriended our own mind, which then trusts that this is a good path that will benefit us all. Although Buddhism is concerned with overcoming the ego and seeing through the delusion of the ego, we can't overcome the ego by beating it to death. It simply doesn't work. Some religious traditions try to do that, but all we end up with is a bitter, unhappy negative ego; it doesn't die from being hit. We dissolve the ego by seeing through it, and this comes about by cultivating an introspective practice.

In order to cultivate an introspective practice, we first have to tame the mind. That means the mind has to become trusting and *want* to cooperate. In other words, right at the beginning the ego needs to be willing to cooperate. Our problem is often that our aspirations go one way, but our selfish desires go another way. For example, when we wake up and remember it is time to get up and meditate, we can think *Oh, meditation is fun; let's meditate.* Then there isn't an inner battle between one's higher aspirations thinking, *Now it is time to meditate*, and the ego thinking, *No it is not; it is time to turn round and go back to sleep.* Instead, they need to work together.

In all honesty it does not say this in Buddhist books, but actually when the ego becomes more tamed and begins to cooperate, gaining enthusiasm for the path, this is an enormous step forward. Which is why the Buddha said that first we give loving-kindness and compassion to ourselves. First we calm our minds, and the ego begins to trust the path, even though this path is ultimately the death of the ego. Ironically the ego will help toward its own annihilation because something inside us knows that this will open into something so much greater than the mere ego can imagine.

However, if we are fighting the ego all the time, we are going to have endless problems. We need to get all levels of our mind cooperating willingly. This is important. Sometimes Buddhism seems heavy into ego bashing, but on our relative, conceptual level where we are starting to practice, we have to take *everything* we've got onto the path. And that includes our sense of self, which will remain with us anyway until we reach the eighth *bhumi*, or spiritual level. These texts dealing with the transformation of the negative states into positive are not talking about the ultimate nature of the mind, which is unchanging. Our pure awareness is naturally compassionate and wise and doesn't have to be transformed. What Thogme Sangpo is discussing is the egotistic, relative level of mind, with which we all mostly live unless we are really high-level bodhisattvas.

This teaching is how to accept who we are right now and instead of making it into an obstacle, we recognize this as our big opportunity to advance on the path. If we have to start with our sense of self then at least let us try to be a happy, cooperative, kind, sensitive, compassionate being who can travel the path to the point where the whole illusion will dissolve into something so much vaster. While it is important to recognize this is about the conventional or relative level, the relative level is where we are right now. Since we can't just say about our sense of self, our sense of I, *Okay, I don't believe in you! It says in this book that ego is all delusion and it is emptiness anyway, so from now on I'm just going to be empty awareness.* If we could do that it would be lovely, but it just doesn't work. We have to start from where we are and with what we've got and use that as the path, and then there's no problem.

But don't think that these teachings are beginning practices just for ordinary people and not for higher-level bodhisattvas. Just before my guru Khamtrul Rinpoche passed away, he called together his togdens, or yogis, and said, "There is a teaching that I have to give you since now you are ready for it. Come tomorrow and you will receive this special teaching." Of course the togdens were all speculating about what the teaching could possibly be, since, being advanced yogis, they had already received just about everything. Perhaps some hidden Dzogchen text? It would have to be something like that. Then next day they went to see Rinpoche, and what he taught was *The Seven-Point Mind Training,* which is a famous lojong text dealing with taking difficulties and obstacles on the path and transforming the mind through more skilled responses. For Khamtrul Rinpoche, the quintessential message of the Dharma was a text on lojong, not Dzogchen, not the six yogas of Naropa. That was the last teaching he gave at Tashi Jong before he died.

Once we recognize the nature of the mind, then we can practice how to relax in that natural awareness, but until we are high-level bodhisattvas, we are still mainly dealing with the relative level of our mind. Things are happening all the time, and we have to know how to develop skillfulness to take everything onto the path. It makes sense to befriend the ego in a nice way to render it cooperative. Then our thinking is transformed from a greedy and obsessive self-grasping into an open spacious consciousness that places others before itself. Others' happiness is so much more important than our own since we are just one among all the other people. We can rejoice in the happiness of others, which gives us far more happiness than to rejoice only in our own happiness.

Instead of being angry, we cultivate loving-kindness and compassion starting with ourselves. If our heart inside is feeling happy and peaceful, what other people do is not going to worry us nearly as much. It is because we have this anger inside ourselves that we are not dealing with that makes everyone else an enemy. When we give loving-kindness and compassion to ourselves then naturally this is also going to spread out toward others.

Traditionally we think to ourselves, *May I be well and happy. May I be free of suffering. May I be peaceful and at ease.* Recite any slogan that speaks to you and visualize sending loving thoughts to yourself, maybe in the form of light. When you think, "May I be happy" you are sending loving-kindness, and when you think, "May I be free from suffering," you are sending compassion. Even though at first this may seem artificial and contrived, gradually we begin to feel a kind of peacefulness and warmth inside ourselves. We have to forgive ourselves. We have all made mistakes and acted stupidly. So what? We are human beings. If we were perfect, then we wouldn't need a path—we would already have arrived. It is because we have problems, because we have faults, because we've made stupid mistakes that we need a path. Therefore as we accept ourselves we can reach out and forgive others. We can start by befriending ourselves and being a little more tolerant of ourselves, and that will help us be friendlier and more tolerant of others.

To begin, we sit and quiet down the surface of the mind and send loving thoughts to ourselves. After that, we send them to somebody whom we feel particularly loving toward, wishing that they might be well and happy and imagining them well and happy, free from suffering. This is the easiest part—to wish happiness to people (or animals) whom we really care for.

Then we spread this goodwill to somebody we feel neutral about, whom we don't care about one way or the other—the mailman, for example, whom we see every day but usually don't give a thought about. Now, just imagine really wishing them to be happy and free from suffering. Everybody in their heart of hearts wants to feel well and not suffer. As the Buddha said, "To each one, his own self is most dear." We wish that for them, imagine them being happy, imagine all their problems solved, and see them free from suffering—their children attend good college and marry nice people and their partner stays healthy. Everything is really nice; all their worries and problems are resolved, and they are just filled with happiness. Imagine it.

Then we visualize someone whom we don't like or with whom we have problems. Just think of that person and recognize that if people create difficulties for others it is because inside they are not really at peace with themselves. Wish them well and happy, imagine everything they want being fulfilled for them, and all their worries and anxieties, all their problems fading away. They're just happy. Feel pleased for them.

Then just gradually expand that sense of goodwill around the world, thinking of all the many beings out there—not just human beings but animals, insects, birds, fish, all the beings who inhabit this planet, and then all those who inhabit the other realms that we can't even see. Imagine that all these beings finally experience having all their worries and anxieties melt away to be replaced by great happiness and joy and satisfaction. May it be!

This is a powerful meditation that comes down from the time of the Buddha. For example, in Thailand many meditators practice in the jungles where there are many poisonous snakes, tigers, and other wild animals, and these wandering monks don't even live in a hut, they just have a tiny one-man tent made of a mosquito netting and sometimes not even that. But in all these years the animals have never harmed them. Other people, such as the villagers, go into the jungles, and they get bitten by snakes or attacked by tigers; it is common. But the monks are safe because they practice loving-kindness meditation, and the animals can feel that. Usually these animals only hurt people if they sense they themselves are going to be harmed, and they know that these beings sitting there are not going to harm them. Since these monks practice nonviolence, these wild animals become peaceful in their presence. There are many stories of monks coming out of their meditation and finding themselves faced with a cobra or a tiger sitting there gazing at them tranquilly.

Typically, if we don't harm others, on the whole they usually don't harm us. When I was living up in the mountains in Lahaul, there was a pack of wolves that looked like large German shepherds with yellow eyes. Sometimes when I was sitting outside they would come close but be just friendly and curious. They would stand there looking at me, and I looked at them, and it didn't occur to any of us to feel threatened. Actually, I have always liked wolves, so it didn't even come into my mind to fear them. At night they would gather above my cave and howl. It is very beautiful, the howl of wolves.

Because there's so much negative energy in the world, it's good to send out positive energy as often as we can. Perhaps while we are sitting in the plane or on the train, we could practice loving-kindness meditation, or tonglen. We don't have to change our posture; we can just send out thoughts of loving-kindness. Imagine beautiful light radiating to fill the cabin and being absorbed into the cells of the passengers' bodies, taking away their suffering and replacing it with light and love and happiness.

21

Dropping Greed

Sense pleasures and desirable things are like saltwater—
The more one tastes them, the more one's thirst increases.
To abandon promptly
All objects which arouse attachment is the practice of a
bodhisattva.

THE BUDDHA HIMSELF SAID that greed is like salty water; the more we drink, the thirstier we become. Even if we drank the whole ocean, we would still be thirsty. The same is true for our modern consumer society. People now have so much beyond what they could have imagined even fifty years ago, and yet they are still not satisfied. They are just endlessly grasping. And for what? The point is that it all becomes counterproductive after a while. We get one car, and it is exciting, but the second car is somehow less interesting, and by the time we get to our fifth or sixth, who cares? We've just got to worry about where to park all of them. Even though the more one tastes, the more one's hunger increases, this desire has diminishing returns. We are always hoping to regain that initial sense of satisfaction. There is a moment of feeling real pleasure and then it is gone. Like ice cream that is delicious at first, but if we keep eating the whole container then we feel sick.

After the initial moment of pleasure the feeling of satisfaction lessens, so then we try something else and then something else . . . we always need something more. It is like pornography that gets increasingly explicit, gross, and vicious in order to help viewers regain that frisson of excitement and pleasure. There always has to be more and more until one is enslaved. It becomes an obsession, an addiction, which is sad.

Sometimes greed seems harmless compared to hatred and jealousy. Around the world people are always asking how to get rid of anger, but few people ask how to overcome greed, because greed appears innocuous and seems quite pleasurable. Anger on the other hand doesn't give real enjoyment, and angry people are unpopular. Being greedy and attached appears natural and the way to happiness. But the root of duhkha, of suffering, is *not* anger. The root of suffering is clinging and attachment.

When I lived in Lahaul, outside the front of my cave was a flat space, like a small patio made of stamped earth, that would turn into mud whenever it snowed or rained. I decided to collect many flat stones to put down on this ground so it wouldn't be so muddy. But on this hard-earth patio grew little clusters of pale pink flowers with yellow centers. They were very pretty, but nonetheless, I thought that I had better pull them up because otherwise the stones would not settle properly. First I tried just pulling them up, but they wouldn't come because the roots were deep, so I started digging to find the taproots. I dug and I dug and I realized, after several days of work, that all these little flower clusters were connected underneath by a deep root system that spread deep and wide in all directions. Yet on the surface all one saw were these pretty little flowers.

At the time I thought that this is like greed or desire. It looks so innocent on the surface, but underneath in the psyche it has deep, thick roots reaching throughout all the levels of our consciousness. Because it is "underground," buried in the subconscious, or store consciousness, we don't recognize it. But this is why it is so difficult to uproot. Anger is relatively easy to deal with because we don't like it, and so we are happy to work on trying to overcome it. But greed is difficult to uproot because we are attached to attachment.

Most people don't understand what it means to transform attachment into genuine love. To uproot attachment doesn't mean that we stop loving. It means that our love becomes purified because it is not tied up with attachment. Mostly what we think of as love is really just grasping or clinging, and it is this grasping mind that causes us suffering. It is deeply embedded in our psyche.

This doesn't mean that we have to give up everything or outwardly renounce the things that we love, but we can renounce them inwardly. In other words, we can have possessions and appreciate and enjoy them, but if we lose them, we don't care much, we can let them go. The test of whether we are attached or not is how we feel if we lose something or someone we love. Are we holding on with both hands or are willing to let go? Inwardly, we need to be able to let go. It's only when we grasp tightly that we have a problem. And truly on the wheel of birth and death, there are no chains, there are no ropes that tie us to anything or anyone.

There's a story about a way of capturing monkeys in Indonesia—whether it's true or not I don't know. Fixed to a tree is a coconut with a small hole bored in it, just big enough for a monkey to put its paw through. Inside there is some sweetened coconut. The monkey comes along, smells the coconut, puts its paw through and grasps the sweet coconut. Now it has made a fist and the hole is too small for the fist to pull back through. Then the hunter comes along, and the monkey is terrified, but the greed in the monkey's mind overcomes its fear and it still cannot let go. The monkey wants desperately to escape, but it also wants to have the coconut. It is caught. That's our predicament, too, isn't it? Yes, absolutely we want to be free—but we want to take everything with us too.

To abandon all objects that arouse attachment doesn't mean that we have necessarily to give away everything, but it does mean that we should look carefully at what we are really attached to. There's nothing wrong with appreciating and enjoying something. Likewise with people, to love and care for them and do one's best to make them happy is not the problem. It is the grasping that is the problem. The idea that now they are *mine*.

So the easiest way is just to let it all go, like the Buddha did. We leave our homes and families and off we go. The more subtle way is not to leave but to work on the ability to hold things gently and caringly but without grasping. That's much more difficult, but if we can do that, then inwardly we become free. Somebody said that if there were only one mantra in Buddhism it would be "Let Go!" Outwardly we can have everything, but inwardly we need to let go. It is not the things themselves; they are innocent. It is our attitude to the things that is the problem. "To know how to be satisfied with what you have," Dilgo Khyentse Rinpoche said in explaining this verse, "is to possess true wealth. The great saints and hermits of the past had the ability to be content with whatever they had and with however they lived. They stayed in lonely places, sheltering in caves, sustaining their lives with the barest necessities."[40]

Once we recognize how little we really need, we can let go of the excess. This is why in Buddhism, to help us ordinary worldly people, the first of the six paramitas, or the six transcendent perfections, is generosity—the process of giving and sharing and the pleasure that can be gained from it. In Asia, the main Buddhist practice really is generosity. It is a striking distinction between the West and Asia. In the West the emphasis is on meditation, and in fact Buddhism and meditation are often regarded as the same thing. But in Asia few people actually meditate, even among the monks. It is considered a specialized or professional thing to do. Probably the only Asian country where ordinary people seriously practice would be Myanmar. For various historical reasons the Burmese have in the past 150 years taken up formal meditation practice, so that ordinary village people and army officers and anybody can practice.

But in most of Asia the qualities most cultivated in Buddhism are generosity and devotion, so people take great delight in giving. There are many opportunities for people to cultivate generosity.

Early morning in the Theravada countries, laypeople kneel in the street with food they have cooked to offer to the monks as they go by. There are regular gatherings where they can make offerings to the temple or to each other; they love to make offerings at every opportunity. The joy of giving is important because generosity is one of the main antidotes to grasping. If we have something and we are happy to share it with others, then there is nothing wrong with having it.

So this quality of delight in giving to others is important and is why it is placed at the beginning of our spiritual training. Because even if our ethical conduct is a bit suspect or we get bad tempered quite often or we never meditate and our diligence is weak, still we can be generous and learn to give beyond what feels like our comfort zone. We can practice giving away things we actually like rather than just the stuff that we have outworn or no longer use or something that an aunt gave us last Christmas that we want to get rid of anyway. Open hands are important because open hands lead to an open heart.

Some years ago I knew a swami, or Hindu renunciate, who lived simply in his ashram built with mud bricks and bamboo. Now this swami had a number of affluent disciples who would offer him a lot of fancy goods. He would examine each article and seem so interested in it, and then the next thing one knew, he had given it to somebody else. He didn't have sticky fingers, and when he died he left nothing, but he was always happy. He was pleased that people gave him nice things because then in his mind he was thinking, *Oh, this is really nice, so who would like this? Who can I give this to?*

Developing that kind of intention is a good thing. Delighting in having something so that we can share it with others helps to break down our total absorption in our own pleasure and happiness. It helps to begin loosening those fingers that are grasping so tightly onto the things we desire, which is why the Buddha himself always encouraged people to be generous and kind. It opens up the heart.

Recently a group of Vietnamese people who live in Australia came to visit us. It was their first trip to India, and I had previously met them in Australia when I gave a talk at their temple. Since I left, which was some years ago, they had been saving up to come to India, to go on a pilgrimage and make offerings everywhere. Their whole idea was that coming to India would give them an opportunity to go to certain monasteries to make offerings to all the monks. They had happily deprived themselves of all sorts of things for years, just so they could all come to India together and make offerings. This was beautiful. They weren't planning to save a lot of money so they could stay in five-star hotels; they were just thinking to make more money than they needed to give away as offerings.

So generosity is a direct antidote to our greedy grasping mind that's thinking, *What's in it for me?* Instead of believing that if we accumulate more and more somehow we'll feel satisfied, we recognize that if we give away more and more, we'll feel lighter and deeply content.

22

Embracing the Nondual

All that appears is the work of one's own mind;
The nature of mind is primordially free from
*   conceptual limitations.*
To recognize this nature
And not to entertain concepts of subject and object
*   is the practice of a bodhisattva.*

HERE WE ARE DEALING WITH two aspects of the mind: our
ordinary conceptual thinking and the ultimate nature of the mind,
which is primordial pure awareness (known as *rigpa* in Dzogchen).
Normally as ordinary sentient beings, we are mostly aware of the
conceptual level of the mind, which means our thoughts and emotions, our memories, our judgments, and our ideas and beliefs. As
Dilgo Khyentse Rinpoche points out:

> The many different perceptions of everything around you in
> this life arise in your mind. Look at your relationships with
> others, for example. You perceive some people in a positive
> way—friends, relatives, benefactors, protectors; while there
> are others whom you perceive as enemies—those who criticize
> and defame you, beat, fool or swindle you. The process starts
> with the senses, through which the mind perceives various
> forms, sounds, smells, tastes, and feelings. As it becomes aware
> of those objects outside, it categorizes them. Those that it finds

pleasant it is attracted to, while those that it finds unpleasant it tries to avoid. The mind then suffers from not getting the pleasant things it wants, and from having to experience the unpleasant things it wants to avoid. It is always busy running after some pleasant situation or other that it really wants to enjoy or trying to escape some unwanted one that it finds difficult and unpleasant. But these experiences of things as pleasant or unpleasant are not functions intrinsically belonging to the objects you perceive. They arise only in the mind.[41]

If we ask ourselves, "Who am I?" then we will recall our name and maybe our nationality, racial type, gender, maybe our class or caste, and we think, "This is who I am." We might think of where we were born and where we grew up. We might include our profession or our marital status. We are somebody's child and perhaps someone else's parent. Sometimes we are the boss but at other times we are the servant. We are playing many different roles—including male and female—which we think define who we are even though we are changing all the time, from the moment we were born. We see a small child and in a year's time, we won't recognize him—every single cell of his body will have changed. But still we think it is the same boy.

Every cell in our body changes every seven to ten years, and our thoughts are changing moment to moment. New cells in our brain are coming into being while others are dying away, but still we say, "I am me." We have a strong sense that there is a unique and autonomous "me" at the center of ourselves that never changes, whether we are two months old or two, twenty, fifty, or a hundred years old. It is still "me." My opinions, my ideas, my beliefs, my memories—this is who I am. This is the level of consciousness on which we live. And normally when we meditate, this is the level of consciousness with which we are dealing and trying to tame, to train, to transform.

From a Buddhist point of view, this concept of an autonomous "me" is a fundamental delusion. It is the big mistake that keeps us trapped in samsara. Samsara doesn't exist except through the conceptual mind. All of this work that we have been going through, all these verses, are written from the point of view of a mind that from the very beginning is mistaking the rope for a snake. Therefore, this verse is important—in the middle of the text, suddenly BOOM, he lands a bombshell there.

When the Buddha said that there is no self, which we Buddhists call the truth of *anatman*, he wasn't meaning that we don't exist. Of course we exist. But fundamentally we do not exist in the way we conceive ourselves to exist. Consider a table made of wood. This table looks solid today, and when we look at it again tomorrow, it will still be a table, and it will still be solid. Nonetheless we know that from the point of view of quantum physics, for example, the table does not exist at all as it appears. In fact, it is energy/space, not really solid at all. If we analyze the "tableness" of the table, we can never find it.

I remember when I was a schoolgirl studying physics for the first time, I was really interested in what remained when everything was reduced to its ultimate level. What is the final reality when we keep reducing everything down? I asked the physics teacher, and she went on about protons and neutrons. But I thought, no, if there are protons or neutrons then those must be capable of being split further, so then what? I lost interest in physics at that point. I might have been a great physicist, but my enthusiasm was quenched at the age of eleven when I decided to look elsewhere for the answer. But, of course, quantum physicists are intrigued by this question: when we keep reducing everything down, ultimately, what do we get? Apparently they can't find any ultimate. Waves or particles, energy or space, but then what is space? Ultimately there seems to be light and energy; matter is not really solid. We really don't end up with a solid table, and yet it is definitely a table supporting the things we place on it, and it would give us a deep bruise if we ran into it.

On the ultimate level the table is not as we perceive it with our sensory perceptions on this vibrational level where we experience the world. There are these two simultaneous aspects that exist all the time. When the Buddha said that ultimately we have no self, he didn't mean that we don't exist but that when we look for this self—this hardcore sense of "me" at the center of our being—we can never find it. It is like peeling the layers of an onion layer after layer but never finding a core.

Likewise, we can uncover layer after layer of the mind until we get down to the substratum consciousness, which in Sanskrit is called the *alayavijnana*. Here our consciousness becomes vast and spacious, and we feel one with everything. Although profound, that kind of feeling is not the ultimate. Through shamatha meditation we can reach that deep level, which is beyond conceptual thinking: the mind feels clear, vast, and blissful, so we can think that we are liberated.

When the Buddha first left his palace, he went to a teacher who taught him how to attain the various *rupa dhyanas*, or levels of meditative concentration, which become increasingly subtle. Then his second teacher taught him the formless concentrations, or *arupa* dhyanas, leading to ultimate nothingness, vast and spacious consciousness, which in his day was regarded as liberation. Even today many people attain this level of meditative absorption and believe they are liberated since it is blissful and spacious. However, Buddha realized that since one has to come back down from that level, it is also impermanent just like everything else and therefore is not the ultimate.

The levels of the mind can be subtle, but they're still caught within this same cycle of samsara. When the Buddha said there is no self, perhaps what he was saying was that this thinking mind and all these levels of meditational absorptions are still caught up within the realm of impermanence of birth and death. They are not liberation. Because when we emerge from that blissful state, here we are again. So what to do?

All that appears is the workings of one's own mind. We only perceive what is received through the sense doors. Normally we believe that objects and people exist out there, more or less how we perceive them. Our senses—especially our eyes and our ears—receive information of what is happening out there, and the brain decodes it nicely so we then can decide how we feel about it. Everything is just how it appears to be.

Only it is not. It is hard for us to realize this. Intellectually it is fairly easy to comprehend, but to actually experience this way of being is difficult because we are already preprogrammed.

Here's a simple example. I worked for a short time in a government office that arranged for candidates to receive vocational training. If someone was going to train to be an electrician, they had to know the difference between the red and green wires. There was a book devised by a Japanese expert, which showed circles of red and green in certain formations. When one looked it was obvious that the circles formed an "A" or a "K." However, in the office was a young man who was color blind, and I discussed this book with him. He said that he only saw whorls of colored circles. He could not make out any letters. There was a girl in the office wearing a fire-engine red sweater. I said, "What color is she wearing?" There was a long pause, and then he said, "I think it must be . . . red?" In fact, he saw a kind of mud color.

So that is an example of how, depending on our ocular perception, we observe different things. Therefore we can conclude that if the color that looks to normal eyesight is actually inherently red or green, then everybody would have to see the same thing. In other words, the color is not inherent in the thing itself but has to do with its vibrational frequencies and perception. Apparently an eminent neuroscientist in England has stated that what we actually see is a blurred image of something, which is instantly interpreted by the brain depending on prior associations. This gives us a picture that we think is a true representation of what we are perceiving. He said that only about 15 percent is received through the sense doors, and something like 85 percent of what we think we perceive is actually made up by the brain.

As such, all that appears is the work of one's own mind. We see things, and we think that's exactly how they are, but of course, it is only how *we* see it. Dogs perceive things differently. For instance, they have one million times the capacity of olfactory experience than we do, which is why dogs are so fascinated by smell. Their sense of smell is so acute that they live in a world of scent, which we don't share at all.

There are people who have extremely acute hearing, while others only hear sounds within a narrow range of frequencies. And there are those who don't have as broad a color range as we have, and still others who have a greater range. We only perceive what our senses can receive, and like a computer the brain interprets the information rapidly, works it all out, and comes up with a picture for us. What is actually out there? We can never know since it all depends on the sense organs and brain mechanisms innate to human beings, and even these functions have unique individual capacities.

The rest is just our preconceptions, our judgments, and tastes— what we like and what we don't like. Sometimes things that a while back were considered beautiful and aesthetically pleasing are now considered ridiculous. We look at old photos and exclaim, "Goodness, did I really wear that?!"

The fact is that we don't really know what's out there. We only know what we perceive with the limited senses we have. If we had different kinds of senses, or extra senses or fewer senses, the picture would change. Even scientists are only using the kind of senses and brain that they have as human beings, so they also have their limitations. We can't imagine what other kinds of senses might be like because we've never had them.

Therefore, on one level, everything that we perceive is our own inner movie show. In fact, we don't even know what's going on in here, to say nothing of what's going on out there. All of our perceptions are gathered and interpreted by the thinking mind, our conceptual mind. But our conceptual mind is dualistic by its very nature. That means it naturally makes a division into subject and object.

When I went to get my first meditation instruction from an old yogi called Togden Choelek Rinpoche, he said to me, "This table, is it empty?"

So I said, "Yes!"

And he said, "Do you see it as empty?"

I said, "Nooo . . ."

"The mind. Is it empty?" he asked.

"Yes!" I said, with a bit more confidence.

"Do you see it as empty?" he countered.

"No," I said.

"Which do you think is easier, to see the table as empty or your mind as empty?" he challenged.

"Oh, the mind," I replied.

Then he said, "Okay, you belong to us."

So I asked, "And if I had said the table?"

He said, "Then I'd have sent you to Sera Monastery down the road!"

This conversation shows that the scholastic approach is to analyze the emptiness of external phenomena, while the yogic tradition is to examine the emptiness of mind. The mind is empty by nature. What does that mean? The classical description is that all phenomena are empty of inherent existence, which means that we cannot find anything existing independently and say that this is the thing itself, whether a table or the mind or anything else. We can never find the actual thing itself. Everything is made up of bits and pieces put together and labeled.

Where is the tableness of a table? It cannot be found. After all, anything can be used as a table if it is slightly flat. We use another object as a table and say, "Now, this is a table." Yesterday maybe it was a box, but today it is a table.

Even though that is a simplistic explanation of a profound understanding, it is an important one, because we do label everything and then believe our labels instead of recognizing that this is just a label, just a convenience.

The Buddha said, "I, too, use conceptual language, but I am not fooled by it."

And that's the difference: we are fooled by it, and we think that if we give something a name, it exists as a separate, independent entity.

But here we are dealing specifically with the mind, not tables, and so the point is, what is the mind? Why is the mind empty?

First of all, the mind is empty because our thoughts are flowing endlessly, like bubbles swept along in a stream. We cannot pick one up and say, "This is the mind" or even "This is a thought" because the moment we identify it, it is gone. Anyone who has tried looking at the mind can see that when we say, "thinking," we can never find the thought itself. It is like the frames of a movie moving across the projector so fast that they seem to project out this whole drama. Each individual frame is moving too fast to be identified. By the time we've noticed it, it is gone.

The mind's emptiness also connotes its spacious quality. The mind is empty but also luminous or cognizant. Mind is not something graspable—it is something vast and open, luminous, clear, and knowing. The nature of the mind is compared to the sky. If we look at our mind, we realize that there are two processes going on: There are the thoughts coming up and disappearing, moment to moment, just flowing past. Then there's awareness—the mindfulness that observes the thoughts. Now that observation is already a step forward. Normally we are just engulfed in the flow of thinking and swept along by our thoughts. But now we are stepping back and observing the thoughts, so there is a space between the observer and the thoughts.

However, that is still a dualistic situation, because there is the observer and the observed. This observing mind is called "mind-fulness." We are now conscious of our mind and in being more conscious, we are no longer so completely enslaved. We can begin to see that all these feelings, these thoughts, these ideas, these beliefs, these memories, prejudices, judgments, and clinging are just thoughts. Merely thoughts.

So here we are, observing the mind. Watching the thoughts as they go past, recognizing that thought moments come and go. In the beginning the stream of thoughts is like a waterfall cascading down. Then it becomes like a fast-flowing river, gradually moving more slowly as the mind quiets down until, eventually, it enters the ocean of samadhi.

This is the conventional mind. That mindfulness that watches is also the conventional mind. Think of the clouds in the sky during a rainstorm. The sky is completely covered by clouds; only clouds are visible. Likewise, the nature of the mind is covered by all our conceptual thinking and, therefore, when we look at the mind, all we see are the clouds of conceptual thought.

But those clouds could not exist if it were not for the sky. The clouds come from the sky, and they vanish back into the sky again. But we usually identify with the clouds. When the clouds part, we see the sky. It is rather like flying in a plane through thick clouds until suddenly the plane ascends, and we are above the clouds and there's this vast blue expanse with the clouds below. Clouds float within this open spaciousness, which is empty. It is empty insofar as we cannot grasp it, it cannot be seen. Yet without space nothing would exist. Space is everywhere. Where is space not?

If we are asked to describe a room, then we will refer to the furniture, decorations, and any people present. But what is really there is space. But we usually don't notice that. Yet without the space there could be no furnishings, there could be no people. Furnishings and people can only exist because there's space.

Also the people and the furniture themselves are ultimately space. Every cell in our body is space. If the physical body is reduced infinitely there are perhaps just vibrations of light. We are all space. There is nowhere that space is not. It is all-encompassing.

Therefore, the nature of the mind is compared to space and is likened to the sky. Mindfulness is a good step in advance of being completely engulfed in our thinking, yet even our mindfulness is based on the sense of my mindfulness. It has not transcended the subject and object duality. There's mindfulness and something to be mindful of. But the ultimate nature of the mind is like the sky because it cannot be divided. There's no center, there's no end.

When we talk about Buddha-nature it could sound like everybody's got a little Buddha sitting inside them. "This is my Buddha." "Keep your Buddha to yourself." "Actually, my Buddha is rather a special Buddha compared to an ordinary person's Buddha!" It is not like that. It is not like everybody has a little Buddha-nature sitting inside them. That would just be another ego projection.

Buddha-nature is empty. Buddha-nature is like space. We can't grasp space. We can fight over our particular seat in a room, but we cannot argue about the air. We are all sitting here, breathing in and breathing out the same air. I cannot say, "Excuse me, I don't want you breathing my air!" Even if we were the bitterest enemies, fighting and shouting at each other, we are actually intimately connected because we are breathing in and breathing out the same air, which descends deep into our lungs.

We cannot own air. Air is something shared by all the beings on this planet, not just human beings. Animals, too, and the trees and the plants are also breathing in and breathing out, helping us to live on this planet. Space has no center, and it has no boundaries; it just is—vast empty space like the true nature of our mind. But, unlike the sky, which is just empty, the nature of the mind is also cognizant. It knows.

The Tibetan word often used to describe one aspect of the true nature of the mind is *sal,* which is a hard word to translate into English. *Sal* means "clear" and also "bright," "luminous." It also has the connotation of being cognizant. The mind is empty—meaning it is spacious, open, unimpeded, and ungraspable—and at the same time the mind is clear and luminous. The mind is naturally cognizant.

If it weren't, we could not know anything, we could not be aware—but we all know. The Tibetan term *rigpa* (or the Sanskrit term *vidya*) means "to know," but it is usually translated as "pure awareness" or "primordial awareness." It is the fact that we know and that knowing is unimpeded, spacious, clear, and luminous—and it is who we are.

But that knowing quality of the mind, which we all possess and is right here all the time, is beyond duality, meaning when we are in a state of rigpa there is no sense of "me" and "others." Such duality just does not exist. It is not that we are spaced out; it is more like we are waking up. The word *buddha* is from the root *buddh,* which means "to awaken." And it is just like that—we suddenly wake up.

We are able to see and hear things because we have awareness. But when we see or hear something, we immediately superimpose on it our ideas and judgments, so that the underlying clarity is obscured. The luminous clarity is always present, but we cover it up with all our dualistic thinking. We don't allow our mind to remain in its naked awareness, which is its natural state before we clothe it in all our concepts.

Without this underlying awareness we couldn't exist. But we are so busy thinking, comparing, conceiving, judging, and talking to ourselves that we don't recognize it.

The aim is to recognize this fundamental quality of the mind. My lama said to me, "Once you recognize the nature of the mind, then you can start to meditate." Meaning that until then, we are just playing mind games.

Once we experience the initial breakthrough, we understand what we are trying to do. Then building on that, we learn how to stabilize that realization. Normally, even if we recognize the nature of the mind, then immediately the dualistic mind goes, *Hold on! That's it! Finally I've got it—now I'm enlightened!* The ego immediately grabs onto the experience and wants to reproduce it.

Many people, when they first start to meditate, have no preconceptions: their minds are innocent. They have no ideas about what's supposed to happen, and they just sit there. They have been told to recite a mantra or follow their breath or whatever, and because their mind is so relaxed, with no expectations and no goals, some experience might spontaneously happen. It seems so easy! They think, *Wow, that's fantastic! Let's do that again!* And then it doesn't come, because now the mind is grasping and wanting to replay that experience. As soon as the mind has expectations and grasps at hopes and fears, the door will close. This is what can make this type of meditation difficult. The way to recognize the nature of the mind is to completely relax but at the same time remain focused.

Great masters, who even as children had received deep experiences and understanding, nonetheless spent the rest of their lives practicing. It is necessary not just to recognize the nature of the mind but then to rest within that awareness under all circumstances. Not just when we are in retreat, but in all situations, wherever we are and whatever we are doing.

When one can stay in a state of pure awareness at all times, including during sleep, then the practice is stable. Of course, many great practitioners of all traditions at the time of death go into a state that is called *thukdam*. This means that although their body and brain have ceased functioning, the subtle consciousness, the clear light nature, remains in the body at the heart center. The body does not decay or collapse; it doesn't go into rigor mortis. Actually, it often becomes more beautiful. Practitioners stay in that state for hours, days, and sometimes weeks. This is really quite common. In fact, it is expected of people who have really done any kind of practice that at the time of death they will at least go into a state of thukdam.

The clear light nature of the mind appears powerfully at the time of death, and these practitioners have united completely with that, because they are already familiar with this clear light through their prior practice. They say it is like a child recognizing its mother. If we are not familiar with it, then when the clear light nature of death arises we are startled, and then we have lost it.

Anyway, the point is that ultimately most of this text addresses how to deal with the mind on a relative level—how to handle our ordinary conceptual thoughts and responses and emotions under difficult circumstances. But then in a flash, Thogme suddenly comes up with this verse on the ultimate nature of the mind: "All that appears is the work of one's own mind."

This idea that people are hostile to us, are friendly to us, are saying nasty things about us, or are not being grateful for how kind we've been to them is ultimately the work of our own mind . . . It is all about how we see it. Our ordinary conceptual thinking narrows everything, puts everything into boxes. But the nature of the mind is far beyond all that—it cannot be put into a box. The nature of the mind is primordially free from conceptual limitations—like space.

So it is vital to recognize this nature, not just think about it. In fact, we can't really think about it because then we're still thinking conceptually. This is another point that we should remember: it is difficult to think about something that by its very nature is beyond thought.

Once I saw an interview with a Russian orthodox priest who said that the first thing they were taught at the novitiate is that anything they say or think about God is not God. I thought, *Right on*, because we try to put even the unthinkable into thoughts.

This is why in Tibetan poetry they sometimes start by declaring *Emaho!*, which means "Oh, how fantastic! How wonderful!" It is an expression of wonder. Then the rest of the text reverts back to conceptual language as they try to express the inexpressible. After all, they wrote book after book concerning the inexpressible and then more commentaries on top of that.

It is said to be like a mute person talking about the taste of honey—they can't. They taste the honey, they know what honey tastes like but, being mute and unable to speak, they have no language to describe it. Another example is a documentary about a film team who went to a small island where the people grew cocoa beans to sell to companies who made chocolate. They had never themselves tasted chocolate. They were puzzled about why the companies paid quite a lot for the cocoa beans, so they tried eating the beans and found them to be bitter and nasty. The team asked, "Well, what do you think chocolate is?" The reply came, "We don't know, but they say it is very nice; they say it is sweet and delicious." Then the film crew gave these islanders some actual chocolate, and in the documentary it showed their faces as, for the first time, they ate this delicious chocolate. Then they looked amazed: "Oh, that's what it is all about!" Now they knew for themselves. No need to say anything more. The experience said it all. We can talk and talk about how sweet and creamy chocolate tastes, but the description has nothing to do with how the chocolate tastes when we actually eat it.

This is rather like the nature of mind. We can talk and talk about it, but we are only using conceptual language to talk about something that is beyond concepts. It is like the Zen saying about the finger pointing at the moon. People get fascinated with the finger, but it has nothing to do with the moon. Nonetheless, if we follow the direction the finger is pointing—there's the moon.

So all Buddhist practice is trying to direct us back to the ultimate nature of the mind, which is uncontrived and inexpressible. Buddha hardly ever described Nirvana except to say what it wasn't—for example, to say it was a state without suffering. He didn't talk much about it because the experience is beyond words. If we start talking about something, the mind grasps onto it, and then it thinks it actually knows the thing because intellectually it can discuss it. But we can analyze chocolate—study all the chemical formulae and investigate how it is made—yet we can't really describe its actual taste. The only way to know it is to eat it.

Therefore, this text spends a lot of time on dealing with our ordinary mind, the way it is now and how we can work with it skillfully. Then, from time to time, Thogme just reminds us that our ordinary conceptual mind is not the ultimate, that there is something beyond it.

So like the two wings of a bird, the wisdom aspect and the compassion/skillful means aspect work together. It is not as if once we realize the empty luminous nature of the mind that we then have to forget all the other training in compassion and patience. The two must go together. But in case we start grasping onto the idea that this conventional mind training is the only thing we have to do, there comes the reminder that ultimately it is all empty. As the *Prajnaparamita* says, although we vow to save countless sentient beings, actually there are no sentient beings to be saved. This is because, according to the view of emptiness, what constitutes the sentient being, the sense of self, and separation from others is an illusion. Even though there are no separate sentient beings to be saved, we work to save them, because while that illusion is in place, their suffering is real. We also must ask ourselves, *Who are we to save them since we are not even sentient beings either?* Our own sense of self and separation is an illusion. There is always this play between the two aspects, the ultimate and the relative, and neither side can be discarded. A bird can't fly with just one wing.

23

Recognizing the Illusion

When encountering objects which please us,
To view them like rainbows in summer,
Not ultimately real, however beautiful they appear,
And to relinquish craving and attachment, is the
  practice of a bodhisattva.

WHEN WE SEE SOMETHING that displeases us, we react with
anger and rejection, and the text has been advising us on how
to deal with those situations. However, we not only have to deal
with unpleasant circumstances in life, we also have to be skillful
in coping with pleasant appearances and circumstances, so that we
don't grasp onto them and get attached. One way to avoid grasping
is to recognize the impermanence of all things. Here is what Dilgo
Khyentse Rinpoche says about this verse:

> The outer world and its living inhabitants are all impermanent.
> Your mind and body are together for the time being—but
> the mind is like a guest, and the body like a hotel in which
> that guest will only be making a short stay. Once you truly
> understand that, the seeming reality of your ordinary am-
> bitions will fall away, and you will realize that the really
> meaningful thing to do, for the present and the future, is to
> practice the Dharma.[42]

Again, there's nothing wrong with liking things that are beautiful. We see a rainbow and say, "That's so beautiful!" But we don't grasp it or try to own it. It is not *my* rainbow. And we know that in a few minutes it will be gone. We know that rainbows are made out of space, water moisture in the air, and the sun reflecting in a certain direction. When all these causes and conditions come together, a rainbow appears. We can never find it; we can see it is there, and we can photograph it, yet it is ephemeral. It will last for as long as the causes and conditions come together, and when they're finished, it will fade. We think it is beautiful, and we can appreciate it, as in many cultures the appearance of a rainbow at certain times is regarded as being auspicious. But we don't try to possess it to show to just a few friends. We can't take out a copyright. A rainbow is there for everybody, and part of its beauty is its ephemeral nature.

Likewise, we should try to view all pleasing objects as if they were like rainbows. They're not ultimately real. Although these objects may be beautiful and pleasing, we don't need to grasp or crave. We can just appreciate how beautiful they are—and that's enough. Otherwise, we do not own the objects; the objects own us.

The kind of mind that just sees something with appreciation and joy is an innocent mind. However, when we get ideas of ownership and want to keep things for ourselves, thinking, *This is mine* . . . that's when the problem starts. Even if it is something that we buy because it might be useful, we should recognize that its nature is impermanent, so we don't really *own* it.

We may say, "This is mine," but ultimately what do we own? We don't even own ourselves, how can we own anything else? How can we possess anyone else? At the end of life we leave it all behind anyway. Then what does it matter? It is this grasping mind that is the problem. Not beauty or objects.

Objects are innocent. Objects are just themselves. They haven't done anything; they are not the problem. It is the feelings that they arouse in our avaricious minds that are the problem. It is not that we cannot appreciate things. It is not that we cannot delight in things. But when we reach out and say, "I have to have it . . . now!" that's a problem.

We know we should hold everything lightly. This doesn't mean we can't own anything; it means that we hold it all gently. We appreciate, but we don't grasp. It is the grasping mind that causes a lot of pain. Just as we have to deal skillfully with those things that cause us hurt and anger and upset, likewise we have to deal skillfully with those things that give us pleasure and delight and joy. The aim is to hold everything lightly and gently and just let it all be as it is, allowing things to flow.

This is why generosity is a beautiful quality. Usually we hold on tightly to objects that we like, but with generosity we can hand it on to another, let it go. Then everything becomes lighter; our whole life becomes much lighter. It is amazing how much we grasp at things. One minute it is just an object, the next minute we've bought it, so now it is *ours*, and our attitude has changed completely.

For instance, if we are in an optician's shop and some glasses fall on the ground and break, then we feel indifferent. But when we discover it is *our* glasses that fell on the floor and broke, we get upset: "Oh no! How could somebody have broken my glasses?" As long as it is just glasses, it doesn't matter, but when they are my glasses, then it is a whole different matter. All because of that little word: *my*.

So we should be more conscious. The first step is just to be aware. Be aware that everything is impermanent and like an illusion. We rarely experience anything directly. Everything we perceive or experience is filtered through our dualistic, deluded perception and worldview. If everything we experience is distorted and impermanent, why grasp onto it? Why be attached to it or averse to it? This is why mindfulness is helpful. Mindfulness makes us much more conscious of all this stupid thinking that goes on in our minds that we normally accept without examining and that causes us to grasp onto things that are impermanent and not what they seem. Gradually we become more conscious and more discriminating.

We carry our minds with us everywhere we go. Even if we went to Mars or Jupiter, we would be taking the same mind. This is the mind that we live with, we sleep with, we have chattering to us constantly. It is our most constant companion, staying with us the whole time. Therefore, doesn't it make sense to have a companion who is charming to live with? Would we want a friend who endlessly complains all the time or tells us how useless we are, that we can't do anything right, and are never going to achieve anything anyway? What kind of friend is that? From that point of view, it would be helpful to make friends with our mind. Shantideva praises self-confidence as an indispensable aid for the bodhisattva path. Taming the mind is not only making the mind calm and focused but also friendly and amenable to being trained.

Here we are in our minds, which we could think of like a room where the doors and the windows are usually kept closed. Many people live inwardly, with the curtains drawn or shades down and little light coming in from outside. Meanwhile this mental room is endlessly filling up with lots and lots of junk, becoming a garbage heap of other people's opinions that are constantly aired on television and shared on the internet and in newspapers, books, and magazines. It is rarely sifted through and sorted, and almost nothing is ever thrown out. The mind just becomes like a great junk heap, and we live in the middle of it. Never cleaning or dusting, never opening the door or the windows, never letting in fresh air . . . and then we decide we are going to invite the Dalai Lama home for tea!

Now, if we are going to entertain His Holiness inside, we cannot invite him into a junk heap, so we have to start clearing out. We begin sifting through all this rubbish and deciding what is necessary and what is really not worth keeping. We start throwing out. Open the doors, open the windows, *clean*. Throw out some of this garbage.

Address it by thinking, *What am I doing with this rubbish in my mind? It's just useless. All these judgments, opinions, daydreams, memories . . . a waste of time. Why am I regurgitating all this drama again and again?*

One of the things we discover early on when we start watching our minds is how boring the mind can be. In the beginning it may seem interesting to observe our stream of thoughts, but then it is like watching the same dull drama again and again—yet *another* rerun of *Casablanca*. Yet another story based on distorted perception of our world as permanent and solid when it is impermanent and illusory. Our minds are repetitious and quite boring actually, most of the time. The mind rarely thinks up something fresh and new and exciting. Mostly it is just the same stale material, repeated again and again. The same old grievances and memories—both happy and sad—opinions, ideas, plans, fantasies, and fears. If we start to observe our mind, we see how unoriginal it usually is. Our ordinary conceptual mind is not really very bright. There's a lot of junk in there that could just as well be thrown out—because His Holiness is coming.

So we start to clean away some of the grime, and we begin to decorate with good thoughts, with beautiful thoughts, with original clear thinking. When our mental room is reasonably in order and looking more pleasant, then we can invite His Holiness in. This means we can invite wisdom into our hearts. We can invite wisdom and compassion to come and dwell within us. Actually, His Holiness—the bodhisattva of compassion—doesn't live outside, he lives within us and is the nature of who we really are.

The good news is that we are not this junk, the aversion and attachment, we really are not, and we don't have to always live in a garbage pile. Because that is not our nature. We are all of us so much better than we give ourselves credit for. As the Buddha said, "If it was not possible to do this, I would not ask you to do it. But because it is possible, I'm saying: 'do it.'"

But we can't just depend on an external authority to encourage us. Of course, as with any skill we need guidance and teachers, but ultimately we ourselves must walk the path. At the end of the guru yoga practice, after praying to the lama for blessings, we dissolve the lama into ourselves, recognizing that their mind and our own mind are the same—like water poured into water or a snowflake landing on the still surface of a lake. The two become one. This shows us two things: the rainbow-like nature of ourselves and others and the unity of ourselves and the wisdom mind of the buddhas.

We receive the outer formal direction in order to recognize that the true guide is always within us. The separation is illusory. We should not think that for the rest of our lives we need to always rely on external guidance. Take the word *lama*: *la* means superior and *ma* means mother, so a lama is a "superior mother," and that's the translation of the Sanskrit word *guru*.

When we are little children, our mother takes care of us, trains us, teaches us, and brings us up. Without a mother it is hard for a child. But once we have matured as an adult, if we are still relying on Mommy to do everything for us and tell us what we should do, then Mommy was not a very good mother. The mother should be training the child to become autonomous and independent. Even though as an adult we still love our mother and are grateful to her, and if we have a lot of problems we may go to her for advice, we don't depend on her for everything. A good mother does not encourage her children to become so dependent on her that they are unable to make their own decisions. A superior mother is someone who trains her children to be good, responsible, intelligent, and independent adults.

It is likewise on the spiritual path. Yes, we need guidance, we need instruction, because we are like children spiritually. But, at a certain point, as our understanding deepens, we begin to inwardly grow up, and we need to start trusting our own inner wisdom. There is something within us that knows. Part of us knows that our world is not so solid, that it is impermanent. Usually, it is covered up by all our conceptual thinking. We are so busy talking to ourselves that we can't hear the voice of silence. Therefore, it is important to come back to our original wisdom and trust our own innate knowledge.

While we are still children we rely on our mother and that's important. We shouldn't try to break away from our mother too soon. For example, when I was about six years old, I had this idea that when I traveled with my mother on the bus I wanted to sit separately from her, to show I was independent. My mother always allowed me to sit by myself but, of course, she would be seated where she could keep an eye on me. Even though she allowed me to pretend I was separate and grown up, I knew that she was always there for me. However, in time there was a certain point when I really did want to be separate—and she let me go.

It is the same with gurus. While we are just children, spiritually speaking, we need their guidance, we need their help. But nonetheless the good gurus, the true lamas, train their students not to remain endlessly dependent on them but to learn how to rely on themselves, on their own inner wisdom. If we look at the histories of the great masters of the past, at some point they sent their disciples away. Like Milarepa was sent away by Marpa. He was told to get on with it. Milarepa continued to pray to Marpa, but he didn't see him again except in occasional visions.

Be cautious of lamas who want to have their disciples around them forever; the ones that thirty years down the road still have all their disciples—the same ones. The disciples can't make any decision without running to the lama for his or her advice or consent. That doesn't sound very wholesome psychologically. Does the disciple need the lama or does the lama need the disciple? There is an ancient saying in the Tibetan tradition that, paraphrased, means: In the beginning, the physical teacher as guru. In the middle, the teachings (the texts, practices, and pithy instructions) as guru. Then, ultimately, the true nature as guru.

To wind up discussion of this verse, we should try to view all pleasing objects as if they were like rainbows. They're not permanent or lasting. They are impermanent and momentary. As I said earlier, although the things we are attached to may be beautiful and pleasing, we don't need to grasp or crave. We can just appreciate how beautiful they are. This is true of our relationships too, even our relationship with our teachers or gurus. The kind of mind that experiences everything without attachment is an innocent mind full of appreciation and joy.

24

Letting Go of the Illusion

The various forms of suffering are like the death of one's
   child in a dream:
By clinging to deluded perceptions as real we exhaust
   ourselves.
Therefore, when encountering unfavorable circumstances,
To view them as illusions is the practice of a bodhisattva.

WITH THIS VERSE, Thogme Sangpo suggests that we are fabricating
our own reality and that, because we believe it all so desperately,
we suffer. If we could only see that it is just a projection like a
movie. When we see a film, we laugh if it is a comedy, and we cry
if it is a tragedy. But we remember it is just a show. At the end,
when the heroine dies in the arms of the hero, however much our
heart is hurting at the time, we don't go out wanting to commit
suicide—it is just a movie.

I remember seeing *Bambi* when I was just a little girl. Ah, the
bit where Bambi's mother dies! I only had a mother, and I didn't
know mommies could die. It was a terrible shock. I felt distraught,
torn apart. I cried so loud that my mother had to take me out of
the cinema. We have to be careful about what movies we watch!

"The various forms of suffering are like the death of one's child
in a dream" is Thogme Sangpo's way of telling us to understand
that our experience is one of illusion, or rather a delusion of per-
manence and solidly existing things. If we dream of somebody we

love dying, then in the dream we feel completely traumatized. We cry and on waking up, our pillow is soaked with tears. But then one thinks, *Oh, but that was just a dream.* However, because we think that everything is so real, not realizing that on an ultimate level it is all really our projection, we suffer. This is a hard one for people. But really and truly this is all just a dream. We live in a dream, and we have to wake up. The whole of Buddhism is about waking up from the dream of our ignorance. We solidify everything and we make everything seem so real, so truly existent, but it isn't. It is like a rainbow. It is important that we recognize the illusory and impermanent nature of things. As Dilgo Khyentse Rinpoche points out:

> If you have contemplated the empty nature of all phenomena in your meditation sessions, it is easy to see the dream-like nature of phenomena between sessions. At the same time, you will feel an effortless flow of compassion toward all those who suffer needlessly because they are unaware of the illusory nature of everything.[43]

It is not that we become unfeeling and remote, but that we begin to see from a higher perspective. His Holiness the Dalai Lama is constantly being told awful things that are happening, not only by Tibetans but also by others around the world who come to tell him all the horrible things taking place in their countries. When His Holiness hears these tales of sorrow, he cries. His Holiness is not one of those who think it is not manly to cry. He is happy to weep (so to speak) because he has such an open heart that really empathizes with the sufferings of others. That's the compassion aspect of a bodhisattva.

But then the wisdom side sees that it is all, ultimately, like an empty rainbow. It is always just a projection. And so five minutes later His Holiness is laughing again. It is not because he doesn't care, but because he has the balance of wisdom and compassion so that he can absorb all this suffering, this sadness, and then transmute it so it doesn't sit heavily in his heart.

Because this universal suffering doesn't sit like a huge boulder in his heart, he is not in deep depression all the time or bitter and angry. Instead, all that suffering that he hears about nurtures his compassion and wisdom. Therefore, when people are with him, they feel comforted. They feel an inner joy and a sense that somehow it is all okay. That's part of his power. I was talking with one of his secretaries, and he said that some people go for an audience, and they're tense and upset and angry and crying. They tell His Holiness such terrible things, but then, just by the way His Holiness sits and takes it all in and then gives out his own words of advice—and because of his infinite love and compassion—the visitors come out smiling. Somehow he's taken all the grief into himself and relieved them as though he has taken that burden from them and dissolved it back into primordial emptiness again. He's been doing this for more than fifty years.

We have to bring our pure perception to our experiences and remind ourselves how things really are. Obviously when something really terrible happens, like losing somebody we love very much, naturally we are going to grieve. Nobody is saying don't grieve. But, at a certain point, too much grief dissolves into self-pity. We no longer just pity the one that died or got sick, we pity ourselves. This is also another boost to the ego and doesn't help anybody. It is counterproductive. The ego is happy to be miserable. The ego feeds on our unhappiness as much as our happiness because when something awful has happened, if we are in grief, if we are suffering, then we recall our grief again and again, thinking only about ourselves. This self-absorption is all the ego wants: whether a happy me or miserable me, it doesn't matter—it is *me*.

People who have psychological problems are usually absorbed in themselves. The most sane and healthy people are those who don't think primarily about themselves; they are much more interested in the welfare of others. That gives them a kind of peace and space. Even when difficult situations come up in this world, we have the space to absorb and then to dissolve. There comes a release of such tight grasping. Thogme says:

> Therefore, when encountering unfavorable circumstances,
> To view them as illusions is the practice of a bodhisattva.[44]

We need to be careful to not make these difficulties and tragedies the center of our life and realize that within the extended ongoing movie that is our life, this is just one scene. We need to move on.

It is important to bring wisdom and understanding into our lives. We need to acclimatize our mind beforehand so that when something bad does happen, we have the prior knowledge and strength to deal with it. Buddhist wisdom recognizes that things are not as solid and unchanging as they seem to be, and we need to appreciate that how we see things is only how *we* see things. This doesn't mean that is how things really are, because as we know at this point, we perceive everything through our deluded minds. We do not see things as they really are; only a buddha or Arya bodhisattva sees things truly.

But even if we can't see things as they are, at least we can try to remember that we are not seeing things as they really are. Those with higher wisdom agree that our seeming reality is just a projection. Even if we don't see things that way, we should remember that more advanced teachers, who know much more than we do, are in accord that everything is just a projection. We don't need to grasp onto what is pleasurable or what is painful.

As I mentioned in chapter 1, I was brought up as a Spiritualist, and we had séances at our home in the 1950s, just after the Second World War, which was still very much on people's minds. We had a couple of friends who would come regularly, having lost their only son in the war. He had died when his tank overturned on a bridge and exploded, so the soldiers trapped inside the tank had both burned and drowned. This bereaved couple would come to the séances just to communicate with their son, and he said to them, "Yes, that was horrible, but I'm fine now and I need to go on. Please stop trying to get in contact with me. We had our time together but now let me go, and you carry on with your life." But they couldn't let go of their grief and attachment, because they had centered their whole life around their son—and his loss.

The point is, to lose your only child is a terrible thing, but the movie goes on. He's passed on, and we have to keep going too. To get stuck in that one scene and keep playing it over and over doesn't help anybody. Therefore, whatever awful things happen to us, we have to remember that people are dying and being born all the time. Of course it is horrible, and we wish it hadn't happened, but it *has* happened, and we have to accept that. All these things that come to us can teach us something. What can we learn? It is important to take everything that occurs in our life and try to learn from it.

Some people call this world the schoolhouse of life, and we have some lessons that are hard, but this is how we grow in understanding and experience. If everything was always easy and pleasant, we wouldn't learn that much. Looking back on their life, many people realize that it was during the difficult parts, the challenges, that they felt they actually made some inner progress. Later they feel grateful for that opportunity to grow. Otherwise we just have to keep repeating the same mistakes over and over again until finally we learn the lesson. Once we learn the lesson, we can graduate from that class and go on.

The most potent way to avoid repeating the same mistakes over and over again is to remember that our perceptions of reality (and our own minds) are profoundly mistaken. This is the focus of the final verse of Langri Thangpa's *Eight Verses for Training the Mind*:

May none of this ever be sullied
By thoughts of the eight worldly concerns.
May I see all things as illusions
And, without attachment, gain freedom from bondage.[45]

As you might remember from chapter 12, the eight worldly concerns are gain and loss, pleasure and pain, praise and blame, and fame and obscurity. Most people want to gain and be praised, have pleasure, and enjoy a good reputation. We all want to avoid loss and pain, blame, a bad reputation, and so forth. The point we need to take from this verse is that we should not be caught between these opposites, these worldly aims. Why are we practicing the Dharma? So that people will like us and say nice things about us, and we will be known for our piety? Or so that life will be nice and pleasant and everybody will help us? Those are not good reasons. Likewise, we may do something because we are afraid that if we don't do it, people will criticize us or create problems for us. That is also not a valid motivation. We shouldn't be caught up in gain and loss, pleasure and pain. That is not our motivation.

We certainly shouldn't practice in order to impress others, or because we think people will like us more or for any of these underlying motives of self-aggrandizement. Our intentions for practicing should be purely to be of benefit to others and ourselves, to awaken to the ultimate, and to cherish the well-being of others. That is all.

It is not about inflating our ego. This is important. As human beings, we are all afflicted with self-cherishing thoughts and behaviors, but the point is that we should really dedicate our lives not only to benefiting ourselves but also to benefiting others. However, this doesn't mean that we *only* benefit others and ignore ourselves. There has to be a balance between the two. We have to breathe in as well as breathing out.

If we are only breathing out and hardly breathing in, we are going to be asphyxiated and exhausted quickly. This often happens with people who are in demanding jobs in social work and so forth or in traumatic kinds of professions. They are so kind and compassionate, but they get out of balance and feel guilty if they give themselves any time off or any nurturing. They feel that if they are kind to themselves that is self-cherishing, and they should *only* be thinking of others.

There are those who think only about themselves and couldn't care less about others. They believe that others can take care of themselves and chant the mantra, "It's me that matters to me!" Then there are others who, often because of low self-esteem, feel guilty if they give to themselves. They believe that they must give and give to others and never take care of themselves. That is also an unbalanced way to live, and in the end they just burn out.

It is important that we take care of ourselves so that we are able to be strong in taking care of others. It is like a glass of water: if we keep pouring out the water and never fill up, it is soon going to be an empty glass. It has to be constantly refilled to have something to pour out. Or, if we use our smartphones constantly and never recharge them, then the battery is going to run out of energy. A lot of people also run out of energy because they forget to recharge. We need to recharge our batteries by doing retreats or other things that help us to relax, that give us pleasure and make us laugh, because we don't want to take ourselves too seriously. We all want to lighten up, don't we?

The point is in order to walk the path, we have to be balanced. This is why the Buddha said that we start by giving loving-kindness and compassion to ourselves first. This is important. If we don't give loving-kindness to ourselves, how are we going to give genuine loving-kindness to others? First, we fill ourselves with love.

The Dharma is good at ego bashing. The texts are always going on about the dangers of the ego, of identifying with the self and the self-cherishing mind and so forth. On the whole, in Buddhist countries, people do not suffer from a crisis of low self-esteem. They feel pretty good about themselves; therefore they can afford to take some ego knocks and at the same time be encouraged to put out more effort toward helping others. But for some strange reason in the West, despite the relative affluence and good education, people often have a low and fragile sense of self. But even two and a half millennia ago the Buddha said, "We start with giving loving-kindness, compassion, and empathetic joy to ourselves."

Now, who are we giving loving-kindness to? To the ultimate reality of our Buddha-nature? But Buddha-nature already is loving-kindness. To whom are we sending the love and who is doing the sending? Well, I am sending loving-kindness to me. Here we are dealing with conventional reality, the dualistic mind that creates the illusion of self and other. Even though ultimately the ego is an illusion, in the meantime we need to have a confident sense of self in order to walk the path to the dissolution of the self. Merely saying, "I have no ego" does not help. Who is saying, "I have no ego"? It is the ego! Who is beating down our ego every time it tries to rear its head? Again, it is the ego. This is important to understand. The Buddha saw it clearly. He didn't exactly expound it this way, but if we look at his path, it starts with shamatha meditation, which is practiced to make the mind quiet, calm, and centered. The mind needs to be balanced and healthy in order to enter into the various levels of meditation absorption called the dhyanas. Shamatha is for healing the mind, for getting all our psychological factors well-balanced so that with vipashyana, or insight, we are able to unpeel the consciousness like an onion, layer by layer.

If our sense of self is unhealthy and in pain, we cannot take off the layers. It would be actually psychologically destructive to do so. We have to be strong with calmness and lucid awareness in order to direct that laser beam of insight into the nature of our empty, luminous mind. Therefore, it is important to take these texts in context. The real message of lojong is that even difficulties can be helpful and useful. We gain inner strength from recognizing that all the challenges that we face are a means for us to spiritually progress and to inwardly mature.

If we are happy when things go right, and depressed and frustrated when things go wrong, or we are all loving and sweetness when people do things we like and get angry when people do things we don't like, then essentially we are still at the level of a two-year-old. Two-year-olds are all smiles and dimples when things go the way they want them, and they have temper tantrums the minute they don't. Meanwhile we grow up, and we get older and gain more wrinkles, but inside we are basically still two-year-olds. When things go right, we are nice and friendly. When things do not go right, we get all upset and angry and depressed. We are still having temper tantrums inside, even though outwardly we might be taking deep breaths. We might not display our emotions like children anymore, but inwardly the same reaction is going on: happy when people do what we want, upset when they don't. Just like small children.

The Buddha always said on the Dharma path we have to mature, we have to grow up, we have to become adults. All of these practices are for helping us transform our normal responses and attitude of when things go right, that's good, when things are difficult, that's bad. Maybe those things that we call difficult and bad are the best things that could have happened to us. As I say, this is not just some kind of feel-good New Age philosophy. This is basic Buddha Dharma. Only the ego is deciding whether something is good or not good, based on the pleasure/pain principle. But the ego is ignorant. Sometimes the worst things have actually turned out to be the best things.

"May I understand all things as illusions and without attachment gain freedom from bondage," Langri Thangpa writes. The world that we perceive as being so real and as being separate from ourselves is compared in the traditional texts to an illusion; it is like a dream, like a mirage, like a rainbow, and so forth. In other words, things appear to be exactly as they are, but actually when examined closely, they have no self-existence. Phenomena come together because of causes and conditions, but in themselves they have no ultimate reality. What we perceive are projections from our consciousness. Again, this doesn't mean we don't exist at all. Obviously we do, but we don't exist the way we think we exist.

Recently, I met with a neuroscientist who said that almost everything that appears in our consciousness as a reality isn't real. Nowadays, neuroscientists are finding that the percentage of what our brain mechanism adds to the bare input that comes through our sense doors is actually much greater than first thought. Our seeming reality is brilliantly fabricated by our mind in accordance with the kind of brain, sense organs, and karma that we have and share as human beings. If we had different sense organs and a different brain mechanism, we would see things differently. The Buddha himself said that the universe is created by all the karma of the beings that inhabit it. In other words, everybody is spontaneously creating their own universe.

Neuroscience is now confirming wisdom that has been known for thousands of years in India. What we perceive does not exist in and of itself. For example, when we are dreaming, if that dream is vivid, then we really believe it and our body also believes it. If it is a frightening dream, our heart will pound and so forth. When dogs dream of chasing or running away from something, their legs perform the actions even though they are asleep. Our body believes the dream that the mind is having, but when we wake up, we think, *Oh, that was just a dream. Now this is real.* But from the point of view of ultimate reality this is still just a dream. When we wake to our primordial nondual awareness, nirvanic consciousness, Buddha-nature, dharmakaya, whatever we want to call it, then the ordinary conceptual thinking consciousness that we normally identify with, dualistic by nature, is completely transcended.

From that point of awakening onward, we see things how they really are rather than how they are presented to us through our conceptual thinking mind, which splits perception into subject and object. As we discussed in an earlier chapter, the word *buddha* means to awaken. Although we often translate *bodhi* as enlightenment, it really means to wake up. What we are trying to do is wake up from the dream of ignorance, of our illusion, of our not seeing things as they really are. All Buddhist schools are concerned with how to wake up in order to be free and, at the same time, how to open up the heart to embrace all beings with loving-kindness and compassion.

When we see things as they really are, there is no ego. The ego is creating the movie that we believe is real and then get attached to. Once we realize the movie is just a movie, we are no longer attached. Whatever happens, whether we laugh or cry, it is all just our projection. It is not ultimately real, and we are not attached to the outcome. We enjoy the process, but we don't believe it.

So Langri Thangpa says, "May I understand all things as illusions, and without attachment gain freedom from bondage." Bondage is the bondage of the ego. Once we have gone beyond the ego and recognized the ultimate nature of the mind, then we have no attachment, and we are free from the prison house of samsara.

25

Practicing Generosity

*If those who wish for enlightenment must give away even
    their own bodies,
How much more should it be true of material objects?
Therefore, without expectation of result or reward
To give with generosity is the practice of a bodhisattva.*

THE NEXT SIX VERSES describe the practice of the six transcendent perfections, or paramitas, which are generosity, discipline, patience, diligence, concentration, and wisdom. According to Dilgo Khyentse Rinpoche,

> Each of these virtues or qualities is considered to be truly transcendent (a *paramita*) when it has the following four characteristics: (1) It destroys its negative counterpart—for example, generosity destroying miserliness. (2) It is reinforced with wisdom, that is, it is free from all concepts of subject, object, and action. (3) It can result in the fulfillment of all beings' aspirations. (4) It can bring others to the full maturity of their potential.[46]

The path of a bodhisattva as laid out in the six paramitas starts with generosity, because even if we are not very ethical, even if we have a bad temper, even if we're lazy and pretty dull-minded, and we hardly ever meditate, we can at least be generous. Generosity doesn't require any other particular qualities. It is the start. And generosity is important because as we give with our hands, if we give with the right motivation, it starts to open up our hearts.

There's a story of the Buddha meeting with a wealthy man who was an entrenched miser. He would never give even a grain of rice to anyone, even though he was wealthy. The Buddha said, "All right, you take some fruit in your right hand, and you give it to your left hand. Then from your left hand back to your right hand." This demonstrates the idea of picking something up and letting it go. When we pick up a piece of fruit in one hand and pass it to the other, there is a moment between letting the fruit go with one hand and picking it up with the other that the fruit is not ours. This is practicing releasing and giving, which is so important.

We were dealing earlier with the idea that grasping and clinging and attachment is the source of our problems. The direct counterbalance to that is to start giving and sharing, to cultivate the pleasure of making others happy through gifts—not just material gifts but also the gift of time. People have problems so we give them our time by listening to them and maybe trying to help. This is the gift of service. Many work their whole lives helping others or in service to the Dharma. This is all generosity.

It is not necessary to always be thinking, *This is mine, I've got to keep it. If I give it away, what will I do? I will be deprived. Therefore, I have to keep everything for myself.* That is a sad state of mind. Whereas the mind that says, *Oh, this is lovely. I really like this, who can I give it to?* is an open, joyful mind, and everything flows beautifully. Usually people who are generous also find that things come to them, too. Nothing gets stuck; we don't have sticky fingers. Everything comes and then is shared with others.

This is a beautiful way to live. Not only are our hands open, but our heart is open too. For all of us, this answers the question of how to transform our lives from the ordinary worldly idea of accumulating to the spiritual ideal of giving. This is one reason why generosity is the beginning of the bodhisattva path as laid down in the paramitas.

As mentioned before, this is well understood in Asia, where the people's altruistic generosity is overwhelming. People often give more than they can afford and with so much joy. It lightens everything up. This quality of giving, of generosity of heart, is a important one for all of us at whatever level we can manage to incorporate it as our practice. The joy in giving joy to others is a beautiful thing. It really makes the heart sing.

Many Jataka tales that retell past lifetimes of the Buddha recount how the bodhisattva took many animal forms and sacrificed his own life for the sake of others. The great merit that was created in this way was a primary cause for him finally becoming a buddha.

Of course people sometimes think, "Look at me, I'm being so virtuous!" Certainly in Asia, people can start totting up the merit as though they were keeping a merit bank account. In addition to their monetary bank account, they have a merit one too. But the more we think of the merit, the least meritorious it is. It is important to give without expectation of reward. Forget the merit; just give for the joy of giving. Just give because you want to make others happy or because others are in need. Sometimes it is also good to give something just because we really like it a lot, and we can see our attachment to it. Just watch what happens inside when we give it away. Dilgo Khyentse Rinpoche explains this as follows:

> Never hope for anything in return for an act of generosity, and do not expect as a result that in your next life you will be treated well or be happy and prosperous. Generosity is complete in itself; there is no need for any other reward than having made others happy. If you give something motivated by self-interest, the joy you might have felt will be spoilt, and further unhappiness is certain to follow. But giving out of sheer devotion, love, or compassion will bring you a feeling

of great joy, and your gift will create yet more happiness. The motivation behind the act of giving makes all the difference.[47]

Generosity is a beautiful quality. It is a loving, soft, spacious quality, and it is something that all of us need to cultivate. Not just material gifts but also service and care for others. In many ways, just the openness of heart that delights in giving and sharing is already an important component on the spiritual path and also a worldly path. To be happy, we have to have a generous heart. We cannot be genuinely happy with a closed, tight heart that doesn't want to share anything with anybody.

We will close the discussion of this verse with another quote from Dilgo Khyentse Rinpoche's commentary:

> Generosity is the natural expression of a bodhisattva's altruistic mind, free from attachment. A Bodhisattva is clearly aware of the suffering that can be caused by amassing wealth, and by trying to protect and increase it. Should he [or she] ever have any wealth or possessions, his [or her] first thought is to give it all away, using it to make offerings to the Three Jewels [Buddha, Dharma, and Sangha] and to support those who are hungry or without food and shelter.[48]

26

Practicing Discipline

If, lacking discipline, one cannot accomplish one's own good,
It is laughable to think of accomplishing the good of others.
Therefore, to observe discipline
Without samsaric motives is the practice of a bodhisattva.

IF WE WANT TO CULTIVATE A GARDEN, the first thing we have
to do is prepare the soil. We need to dig out a space, pull out the
rocks, pull up the weeds, and add the fertilizer, making sure the
soil is fertile. Then we need to plant good seeds.

Likewise with our spiritual life, when we are trying to cultivate
generosity, patience, meditation, and wisdom, applying ourselves
to study in order to understand and to cultivate a genuine Dharma
life, we need to do the groundwork by first studying the ethical
guidelines. Without those basic principles our practice will not
benefit even ourselves, so how can we be of benefit to others?

The basic five precepts—not killing, not stealing, not misusing
sex, not engaging in false speech, and not destroying our minds
through drugs and alcohol—show us the way to live in this world
harmlessly. They have nothing to do with what we eat or what we
wear. They are not principles that were important in India 2,600
years ago but are no longer relevant or are only relevant in Asia
but not in the West. They are eternal rules of conduct to uphold
our spiritual life, and they are the discipline of the Dharma. Dilgo
Khyentse Rinpoche teaches:

Discipline is the foundation of all Dharma practice. It provides the ground upon which all positive qualities can be cultivated. In the same way that all the oceans and mountains are supported by the underlying mass of the earth, all the practices of the Hinayana, Mahayana, and Vajrayana are supported by the backbone of discipline.[49]

It is like a cup. If we want to pour the elixir of the Dharma, we have to have something to contain it in. We have to have a cup, or a vessel, in which this elixir can be kept so that it doesn't just run all over everywhere and get wasted. This container is our basic ethical conduct, the way we live in this world. When we maintain the basic precepts, any being who comes into our presence knows they have nothing to fear from us. We are not going to hurt or cheat or exploit them. They are safe with us. We are also safe with ourselves because we know that if we maintain the precepts we will not create negative karma—we have promised ourselves and the buddhas to live ethically, simply, and with benevolent purpose.

There are levels of ethical conduct, both lay and monastic, but all of them include these basic five precepts of right living. It doesn't even matter what religion we hold or do not hold as long as we live harmlessly, not only with our body and speech but especially in our mind.

It may happen that at first our mind is running wild with anger or lust, and we are inwardly involved in all sorts of negative scenarios. But if outwardly we appear peaceful and restrained, then we must work to gradually quiet down the mind. If our outward behavior is impeccable, we can more easily sit and meditate because we don't feel guilty about our outer conduct. The precepts always benefit us. And certainly they benefit the world. Without them, it is laughable to say we are practitioners.

Maybe we are not yet bodhisattvas, but we are trying. This is our practice. Practice makes perfect, as they say. If we want to be perfect, we have to practice. One of the most important points is to start from where we are now. We are happy to bring our lives into line with where we are aspiring to go. If we are aiming in one direction, but our conduct goes another way because all our friends are going out and partying or because it is the norm in the kind of society we live in, our efforts are counterproductive.

But when we are practitioners, we are not following the norm. Buddha, 2,600 years ago, said that anyone who practices the Dharma is like a fish swimming upstream, when all the rest of the fish are going downstream. That was in India, in his day. Imagine what he'd say now. Each one of us is responsible for our own life, our own actions, our own speech, and our own mind. No one can do it for us. The five precepts really are a big help to us and act as a reminder of the direction we are trying to go in.

If we lack discipline, we cannot even help ourselves, we cannot even accomplish our own good, because all these actions, like killing, stealing, sexual indulgence, and so forth, hurt us as well as others and create bad karma leading to an unhappy, undisciplined life. We can't talk about benefiting other beings at the same time that we are killing or stealing or lying to them. Therefore, we observe discipline without samsaric motives. We do not do this just so we can gain merit or so that everybody will look at us and say what a good person we are and think, *Wow, how disciplined and what an exemplary Buddhist.*

The point is if we sincerely aspire to travel the path, the sine qua non is an ethical life—whether people know about it or not, approve of it or disapprove, because we know in our heart it is right and in tune with what is true. We uphold the precepts without making a fuss. We will close this discussion of discipline with another quote from Dilgo Khyentse Rinpoche's commentary:

Without discipline there is no way to achieve either the temporary happiness of liberation from suffering or the ultimate bliss of enlightenment. . . . Guard your own discipline, therefore, as carefully as you protect your own eyes. For discipline, if you can keep it, is the source of bliss; but if you transgress it, it becomes a source of suffering.[50]

27

Practicing Patience

For a bodhisattva who desires the joys of virtue,
All who harm him are like a precious treasure.
Therefore, to cultivate patience toward all,
Without resentment, is the practice of a bodhisattva.

THIS IS REALLY WHAT our whole text has been about. There's no need to go into great detail here because the previous verses have covered it well. In short, if we genuinely wish to transform the heart, we welcome people and circumstances that challenge us, create problems for us, and typically would arouse resentment, anger, humiliation, and negative states of mind. Normally, when we meet with situations and people that create these negative feelings in us, we see them as obstacles, but on this path, we welcome them with patience because they provide us with a chance to practice. As Dilgo Khyentse Rinpoche notes:

> To practice the paramita of patience is essential, so that you can never be overcome by anger, hatred and despair. Once you have entered the path of the bodhisattvas, you should in any case have kindness in your heart for all beings, seeing them as your former parents. When people are against you and do you harm, you should have even more love, dedicating all your merit to them and taking all their suffering upon yourself.[51]

It is not like we go out looking for obnoxious people or problems and difficulties. We only need to stay where we are, and they will come. But when they do come, we are wearing the armor of a bodhisattva, so we are not wounded. In this case we welcome them as opportunities to see how far we have gotten on our bodhisattva journey.

Personally, my main area of practice is going to be the Foreign Registration Office (FRO) in India. So, I'm ready. I'm armored. Before I go in, I think, *Right, this is going to be my lojong practice for the day.* Then usually the police officers are quite polite and helpful. These poor guys. What a life they lead, day by day, faced by frantic foreigners anxious about visa extensions. But the thing is, whatever happens to us, how we respond is an indication of how much we have really understood. If we do get upset and angry, then the point is not becoming angry and upset with ourselves because we're angry and upset. We just remind ourselves, *Okay, now I can see this is where I've got some work to do. I'm really grateful because now I understand. Yes, that situation lit up the area that needs to be worked on.* It is not just being pious. How are we going to cultivate patience and tolerance and forbearance if we do not have people and situations on which to practice? Tolerance is a quality essential for Buddhahood.

One time I was at the FRO, and there was a Western monk in front of me. The officer was saying, "Your form is filled out wrong. You didn't put this here."

The monk replied, "Okay, well, I'll just alter it."

"No, no!" the official exclaimed as he tore up the pages and threw them back at the monk. "You do it again." I mean, there were several pages to this form . . .

So the monk said, "Okay, thank you very much. Please give me another set of forms." The officer gave him another set of forms. As the monk turned around, he saw me, grinned, and winked.

Well done! Well done! So, it is possible.

28

Practicing Diligence

*Merely for their own sake, even shravakas and
    pratyekabuddhas
Make efforts like someone whose hair is on fire
    trying to put it out.
Seeing this, for the sake of all beings,
To practice diligence, the source of excellent qualities,
    is the practice of a bodhisattva.*

SHRAVAKAS ARE THOSE WHO are striving for liberation, for Nir-vana. *Pratyekabuddhas* are those who attain Buddhahood by their own means and without sharing what they have understood with others. Both of these are examples of people who are striving ba-sically for their own benefit without particularly thinking in terms of benefiting all beings. Therefore, they are those who are striving for spiritual liberation without arousing bodhichitta. Even to attain that liberation just for themselves they make tremendous effort to extinguish desire, like someone whose "hair is on fire."

The Buddha used this analogy to signify urgency. Consider how we would immediately rush to the source of water to pour on our hair, which is in flames. We wouldn't care what delicious fruit there was on the way, what beautiful people there were about, what fascinating programs were on television. Our only aim would be to put out the fire on our head. We couldn't care less about anything else. Nothing else has greater importance than extinguishing the fire. We practice with that one-pointed focus, and nothing else matters.

If shravakas have that kind of motivation, even just for one person, how much more motivated should those of us who have taken the bodhisattva vow be, who have aroused bodhichitta, the aspiration for enlightenment in order to be of benefit and rescue all other beings! This is such an incredibly vast vision and clearly requires us to make an even greater effort. There's no question; it's intimidating.

In our tradition, the Drukpa Kagyu, they are kind of proud of all their mad yogis, and one of them was called Drukpa Kunley. Drukpa Kunley once went to Lhasa to visit the Jokhang, which is the central temple in Lhasa. He came to the statue of the Jowo Rinpoche, which is the most venerated image of Shakyamuni Buddha in Tibet. The Jowo Rinpoche was gifted to Songtsen Gampo, one of Tibet's early Dharma kings, by one of his queens as part of a marriage dowry. Drukpa Kunley made offerings and bowed down to the Jowo Rinpoche. Then he said, "OK, you and I started at the same time. You became a buddha. I'm still stuck here in samsara. What went wrong? What's the difference between us?" Then he answered himself, "The difference is you made efforts and I was lazy." When people ask, "What is the main obstacle on the path?" I usually say, "Laziness."

Laziness comes in many forms. There is gross laziness, for instance when we don't want to get up in the morning to meditate, or we'd rather watch a movie than go to a Dharma talk. Those are obvious. Then there is the laziness of undermining ourselves, telling ourselves that other people can practice, but we can't. We say to ourselves, *I tried to meditate, but my mind was so wild—obviously, I'm not meant to be a meditator. I try to study, but it is so difficult or I get so bored. Obviously, I'm not meant to study or Other people are kind and selfless, but not me, I've always had a hard time thinking of anybody outside of myself, so clearly I can't do this bodhisattva sort of thing.*

Constantly, we undermine ourselves, we demean ourselves. We cut away at our confidence in our own potential. But it is also an excuse not to make an effort. If we tell ourselves we can't do it, then we feel all right about not trying. Although it looks like humility, or just a lack of confidence, it is actually a subtle form of laziness.

Shantideva said that there is a difference between pride or arrogance, which is a mental defilement, and self-confidence. Without self-confidence, we will never be able to follow the path. It is important to listen to what we are telling ourselves. We are constantly talking to ourselves. Those who have tried to meditate will know that. As soon as we try to quiet the mind down, we become conscious of an endless inner dialogue carrying on inside. What is that dialogue telling us? What are we telling ourselves over and over? Are we encouraging ourselves, inspiring ourselves, thinking, *Well, yes, I have this problem and I have these faults, but never mind. This is what the Dharma is for. The Dharma is for helping us to overcome and transform our faults. So we've got problems. Everybody's got problems. If we were perfect, we wouldn't need the Dharma.*

Or is our mind telling us how we have always been stupid; how we have always failed at everything we've tried; how basically we're not capable of anything; how, if we try practicing Dharma we are not going to succeed, so why bother to even try? Many people's minds are their own worst enemies. To endlessly tell ourselves how hopeless we are is not humility.

The Sanskrit word for a bodhisattva, which means "an enlightened being" or "a spiritual being," was translated into Tibetan as *changchub sempah*. The word for *bodhi* in Tibetan is *changchub*, but the translation of *sempah* is interesting. *Sems* means the "heart-mind." But *sattva*, meaning "a being," was translated as *pawo*, which is a hero or a warrior. *Bodhisattva* was translated in Tibetan to mean "an enlightened warrior" or "a spiritual hero." There is something heroic about that word in Tibetan.

We have to be heroic. We have to be brave. We have to be courageous. We are vowing to attain enlightenment in order to benefit all beings. We can't sit here and say, "Oh, I don't know. I can't meditate. It is very difficult." We have to believe in ourselves. Of course Buddhism is about getting rid of the self, but in the meantime, while we still imagine we have a self, we must cultivate a heroic sense of our potential. As I suggested, we have to use the ego in the service of finally transcending the ego. A weak, sad little ego that is always telling itself how hard life is, and how it can never accomplish anything, is just another form of inverted pride.

Nobody is hopeless because we all have buddha potential. The nature of the mind is completely fine. It may be a little obscured, but when we have good impulses, we know that our true nature is coming out. The negative impulses that we have do not come from our true inborn nature. We just have to uncover who we really are. We can't tell ourselves that we can't do it and use that as an excuse not to try. Anybody can do it if they try hard enough and keep trying.

It is the same with any other skill. Perhaps we are not going to become Rubenstein, but we can learn to play the piano. If we keep practicing, however many times we need to play the scales over and over, hitting the wrong notes, eventually the music will begin to come. But if we give up after the second lesson, then what? We tell ourselves we are not musical when the reality is we have not been diligent, we have been lazy.

Admittedly the analogy of having one's hair on fire may seem somewhat extreme. But nonetheless, as this text has been saying, we should take our life and everything that happens to us and make it our practice. This means that we don't just think of our practice as sitting on our cushion or going to a Dharma course or reading a Dharma book, and the rest of the time is just so much worldly activity where our minds can go in all directions. In fact, everything we do, if we do it with mindfulness and awareness, can be transformed into a practice.

The third kind of laziness is being involved in too many activities, even virtuous ones, as a way to avoid getting down to more focused practice. Those who run Dharma centers or social projects should be conscious of the potential to get so busy in doing what looks like virtuous activities that they forget what they are really trying to do, which is to cultivate and transform the heart-mind. Even if we are working in a Dharma center very devotedly, we still need to make it our practice. Otherwise, all of our hard work is just another form of avoidance. It is avoidance of what is really important, which is the cultivation, the taming, the training, and the transcending of our conceptual mind.

Without effort we accomplish nothing. We all know that. This is an important quality. If we don't make any effort, we are never going to get anywhere. If we want to go from here to the dining hall, we have to get up and walk. If we just sit here thinking, *Oh food, come, come! Oh, food, wonderful food, please come to me!* and we make no effort to go to the food, then what? We starve.

This whole text has been about how to skillfully transform our lives into an ongoing Dharma practice so that nothing is wasted, everything is taken on the path. Whatever we are doing can be an expression of our inner practice. This is why these kinds of texts are so important. They contain precious instructions that we can take with us and use to transform everyday events and encounters into our Dharma practice, our path on the way to Buddhahood. On the outside they look simple, but their meaning is profound.

Once again, we will give Dilgo Khyentse Rinpoche the last word:

> To awaken and to develop all the paramitas, diligence is vital. Diligence is the joyous effort and active determination to carry out positive actions, without any expectations or self-satisfaction.[52]

29

Practicing Concentration

Knowing that through profound insight thoroughly
*   grounded in sustained calm,*
The disturbing emotions are completely conquered,
To practice the concentration which utterly transcends
The four formless states is the practice of a bodhisattva.

IT IS WELL-KNOWN that the basic formula of Buddhist meditation has two parts: shamatha and vipashyana. Dilgo Khyentse Rinpoche outlines the following in his commentary:

Examine body, speech, and mind, and you will find that mind is the most important of the three. If your mind is thoroughly trained in sustained calm and profound insight (shamatha and vipashyana), your body and your speech will naturally follow your mind along the path of liberation.[53]

The first of the two is shamatha, or "calm abiding," which is the practice of getting our minds calm and relaxed but fully attentive. All the turbulence inside begins to abate and slow down. At the same time, we hone and sharpen our concentration to become single-pointed. We aim here to have our attention so focused that wherever we want to place it, there it rests.

We cannot really understand the mind until the surface chatter has quieted down. Normally, when we start to meditate there are many problems, but an obvious one is that the mind is busy and doesn't want to concentrate on where we place it. We want to pay attention to the breath, and so we think of everything but the breath. We bring back the attention to the breath, and a few seconds later we have to bring it back again. And this is the usual situation when initially we try to practice. We just need patience and perseverance. As the mind calms down and becomes centered, it becomes more supple and workable.

Therefore, the Buddha always recommended that we start with shamatha practice first, before doing anything else. As mentioned previously, in advanced shamatha practice, there are levels called the dhyanas, or mental absorptions. There are the four form absorptions and the four formless absorptions, which Thogme Sangpo mentions in this verse. Siddhartha practiced all of them before he became a buddha and then explained that these rarefied "formless" mind states—such as realization of the infinity of space and the infinity of consciousness—are not in and of themselves liberation, because these states are impermanent and still within the cycle of birth, death, and rebirth.

Therefore, in the Tibetan tradition these rarefied states are not emphasized, although to attain the first dhyana is useful because then the mind is unified and able to remain steady. The first dhyana is a meditative state of focus and discernment along with an arising of joy. In that state, our concentration is now tamed, flexible, workable, and malleable, so that whatever we want to do, the mind can cooperate.

Another example is that when we try to concentrate using our ordinary mind, it is like pouring water on wax paper. It just runs off. But once the mind has quieted down, it is like pouring water onto blotting paper. It soaks right in. Then, whatever practice we engage in we become one with immediately and results come quickly.

After having tamed the mind through shamatha practice, it is calm, still, and clear. We are completely focused and at one with what we are doing. We can now use that clear and focused attention to investigate and gain insight into the mind itself. Some people don't like to do this because with shamatha after a while there are few or even no thoughts. It is calm, and the mind feels spacious and clear. We feel we could just sit there blissfully absorbed forever. When people are told that now they have to start thinking and investigating, they fear that this is a step backward. But actually it is not. This is called vipashyana, or clear insight.

We have cleaned and sharpened the mind like a scalpel, so now it is razor sharp. Now we have to start dissecting by directly looking at the mind. What *is* a thought? Where do thoughts come from? Where do they go? Who is thinking? All these many different questions we start asking ourselves inwardly with a great big question mark. We look. If there are no thoughts, we bring some thoughts up to look at them. Then we question them to death. It is an interrogation: Where do you come from? What do you really look like? Where are you going? Where do you normally live? Okay, what's your name? Don't tell me that! C'mon, try again . . .

We look and we look. Then we look at who is looking. In this way, we begin to understand how we live: whatever stimuli we seem to receive from the outside and whatever we are thinking about on the inside is all thought. Everything is based on thoughts: our beliefs, our memories, our identity, our judgments, everything. This is important because people even go to war and kill others and themselves for what they think and believe. It is all based on thoughts. What is thought? We never look. We are so busy looking outside, we forget to look within at who is thinking. Through this method we can finally transcend all of this duality to come back to the nature of the mind itself.

The nature of the mind itself transcends thought, and at the same time it includes and permeates all our mental activities. So it is compared to space, which is out there and also in here and everywhere—where is space not? The nature of the mind, our pure awareness, is vibrant. It is not something static, because it is the knowing aspect of our mind. Whatever happens, that knowing quality, that essential awareness, is there. If it were not there, we would be corpses. But normally, because our primordial awareness is so covered over with all the clouds of our thinking and emotions, we don't actually experience the awareness in itself. In other words, we are not conscious of being conscious, because we are too busy thinking. Once we recognize our true nature, then everything becomes obvious.

To sustain this realization is difficult. It is like waking up for one moment from a dream—*Aha, that was just a dream*—then we fall asleep again. But next time we have kind of an inkling that this is just a dream now. We still have that memory, even though it is not very clear, that there was another level of consciousness called "awake." This is why in Tibetan Buddhism there is an emphasis on dream yoga and lucid dreaming to help us to recognize dreams while we're asleep.

Basically, all our life is just a dream from which we are trying to wake up. Simply to be satisfied with tranquility and going into the dhyanas, or even to be satisfied with just investigating the conceptual mind, is not enough to liberate us. We need to recognize our primordial awareness and then learn how to dwell within that state of nondual presence continually, day and night, waking or sleeping. That is the path.

The nature of primordial awareness is emptiness and lucid cognizance. We know because we are aware. But what is that awareness? What is it? That is what we have to discover.

30

Practicing Wisdom

In the absence of wisdom, perfect enlightenment cannot
  be attained
Through the other five perfections alone.
Therefore, to cultivate wisdom combined with skillful means
And free from the three concepts is the practice of a
  bodhisattva.

BUDDHIST WISDOM is a huge subject, but at the heart of what we mean by the word *wisdom* is an experiential understanding of the empty nature of all things. The main thing we are considering here is why Thogme Sangpo is suggesting that without wisdom, enlightenment cannot be attained by the other five paramitas.

In the context of the five paramitas, merely acquiring generosity, morality, patience, effort, and meditation, based on the concept that it is I who am doing this and therefore not understanding emptiness and no self, will not result in enlightenment. It will result in making lots of merit but, in itself, will not give us the breakthrough.

Therefore it is specified that to attain enlightenment we need to cultivate wisdom along with skillful means, or the five paramitas. And all of these need to be free from what are called the "three concepts." Now to explain the three concepts, here's an example: I give a packet of chocolates to a friend because my friend likes them and I want her to be happy, or maybe even because I am especially attached to chocolates myself and I want to work on my sense of renunciation. Whatever the reason, I give it to her with good motivation. That act of generosity will make merit, or positive karma, and then what I do with the merit is up to me. But this action is caught by three false concepts: (1) there is a subject (the person who is giving), (2) there is an act being performed (giving), and (3) there is a recipient (the friend). There is also the additional belief that all these actually exist just as I think they do. Specifically, the idea of subject, action, and object and the belief in their absolute existence as we conceive it with our conceptual mind bind and capture us. Therefore, that action in itself will still bind us to samsara. Dilgo Khyentse Rinpoche points this out when he says the following:

> A thorough, experiential understanding of emptiness is the only antidote to the belief in an "I," in a truly existing self. Once you recognize emptiness, all your attachment to such a self will vanish without trace. Realization will blaze forth, like a brilliant sun rising in the sky, transforming darkness into light.[54]

The actions of generosity, patience, diligence, discipline, and concentration themselves are good, but in order to become an actual means of opening up to ultimate reality, they need to be joined with wisdom. Otherwise the underlying delusion doesn't free us. It doesn't liberate us because it is still an ego-centered action: *I am virtuous, I am generous, I am patient.* There's always an *I* there, and so those meritorious actions alone cannot liberate; they need to be joined with right view. This means understanding from the beginning that there has ultimately been no one to give, nothing to be given, and no one to receive.

Through this genuine realization of emptiness and the nature of the mind, we will spontaneously perform all these actions without them being joined to the idea of a personal, immutable, solid *me* at the center of everything. We will experience an open spaciousness instead of being trapped in our usual tight, conceptual thinking. This is liberation of the mind and why wisdom is the crown jewel of Buddhism. Without wisdom free from the three concepts of grasping at subject or self, object or other, and action, the five paramitas by themselves will not take us to enlightenment. It could also be said that the other paramitas are the legs and wisdom is the eyes. If we are trying to reach the goal, either we've got the legs to travel, but we can't see where we are going, or we have eyes but no legs, so we are not going to get very far. We need both eyes and legs to travel the path to enlightenment.

31

Examining Oneself

If I do not examine my own defects,
Though outwardly a Dharma practitioner,
  I may act contrary to the Dharma.
Therefore, continuously to examine my own faults
And give them up is the practice of a bodhisattva.

WE HAVE TO LOOK AT our own actions and our own mind. When there are faults, when there are problems, when there are difficulties, we have to acknowledge them. It doesn't mean that we beat ourselves over the head. It doesn't mean we think we are bad people. Rather, it means that we need to get to work on these problems, we need to take our proverbial scrawny legs to the gym and start running on the treadmill!

The point is that we need to see the problem in order to set about remedying it. It is the same as needing to realize that we are sick before we can take the treatment. It is not that we feel guilty or punish ourselves because we have some illness. Once we acknowledge that there is some problem, we then seek to find how to make ourselves spiritually healthy again. Our true nature is health, our true nature is Buddha, but our thoughts and our emotional defilements obscure that truth. We have to heal and remove these obscurations, but not in the sense of getting out the whip and flagellating ourselves. We acknowledge that there are problems, but as it says in the text, we can deal with these problems because there is always a skillful way. That's the work, that's the path. It is nothing to get depressed about. In fact, it is something to get energized about. This is our problem so let's get to work on it now.

Otherwise we can pretend to ourselves, fool ourselves. This is sometimes a problem with people who practice the Dharma. We read all the texts on how perfect bodhisattvas act: they never get upset, they never get angry, and when people cheat them and abuse them, they say, "Oh thank you, my spiritual friend." People read all these texts and think, *That's how a bodhisattva has to act, so I am going to be a bodhisattva and act just like that.* Then we pretend. We play the role of a person who never gets upset and never gets depressed or angry, because bodhisattvas would not do those things. We pretend to ourselves and especially to others that there's no problem and that we are sincere Dharma practitioners—all the while we are suppressing and ignoring all these problems that are growing in the darkness. Many things are growing in the darkness. We need to open up, to expose them to the light. Then they begin to shrivel, and we can see what's going on in there.

It is not virtuous to pretend to be who we are not. While it is skillful to aspire to overcome our problems, it is not wise to pretend that there are no problems to overcome. This is especially true in Dharma centers where everyone is trying so hard to be perfect. None of us is perfect. Of course, we try to do the best we can, but we still have to acknowledge to ourselves when problems arise. If someone upsets us, we have to admit that they upset us. Then we can think about how to deal with the upset in a suitable Dharma way, and we try to do so. But to pretend that we are not upset because bodhisattvas never get upset is just to be in denial. It is psychologically unhealthy behavior, because if we cannot acknowledge the shadow, it grows.

So if we want to come into our true nature, we have to look at our faults and then work to give them up or transform them. We ask ourselves, *What is the best way for me to deal with this problem that*

I have? We search in the texts, ask the teachers, think about it, and finally decide what works for us. Then we do it.

Once more, we will turn to Dilgo Khyentse Rinpoche's commentary on the subject:

> Ordinarily, whatever you do, say or think is an expression of your belief in the true existence both of yourself as an individual and of phenomena as a whole. Your actions, as long as they are based on that false premise, can only be deluded, and permeated by negative emotions. As you follow a teacher, however, you can learn how to keep everything you do with body, speech, and mind in accordance with the Dharma.
>
> Intellectually, you can probably recognize right from wrong, and truth from delusion. But unless you apply that knowledge in practice all the time, there can be no liberation. You have to bring your own wild mind under control by yourself—no one else can do it for you. No one else but you can know when you have fallen into delusion, and when you are free from it. The only way to do that is to keep looking into your own mind, as if you were using a mirror. Just as a mirror enables you to check if your face is dirty, and to see where the dirt is, so, too, being constantly present in every situation and looking within at your own mind allows you to see whether or not your thoughts, words, and deeds are in accordance with the Dharma.[55]

32

Abandoning Criticizing Others

If, impelled by negative emotions, I relate the faults
Of other bodhisattvas, I will myself degenerate.
Therefore, to not talk about the faults of anyone
Who has entered the Mahayana is the practice of a
   bodhisattva.

ON THE WHOLE, to gossip about others and to denigrate others is definitely a nonvirtuous action. It creates disharmony, and often talking about others' faults is a way of avoiding one's own shortcomings. We should always listen carefully to what we are saying—actually hear ourselves speak. We should not say anything about someone else that we would not be happy to say in their presence, whether they are on the Mahayana path or not. Gampopa, the main student of Milarepa, explains at the beginning of his influential text *The Precious Ornament of Liberation*, that because all beings have Buddha-nature, disparaging any of them is inappropriate. Instead, we should all respect one another.

That being said, when we know of someone who is abusing their position, who is acting in ways that are unethical and unacceptable, then, as His Holiness the Dalai Lama himself recommends, we should speak out, if only to protect others. We don't need to make a major issue out of it, but we should speak up, for their sake as well as everyone else's sake. Otherwise if we stay silent or worse, sweep everything under the carpet, put the carpet back down, and think that the room is clean when it isn't, it is a disservice to the person who is abusing their position.

If we don't speak up, they might continue in their corrupt conduct, which is ethically unwholesome and just creating bad karma. Remaining silent or engaging in cover-ups is also a disservice to anyone else who comes under their influence or is harmed by them. It can create an atmosphere of deceit and harm with everyone afraid to speak out honestly. Therefore, sometimes we have to speak out with compassion for both the victims and the perpetrator and to maintain the integrity of the precious path. But be sure of your facts before you do so.

33

Not Profiting from Dharma

Offerings and respect may bring discord
And cause listening, reflection, and meditation to decline.
Therefore, to avoid attachment
To the homes of friends and benefactors is the practice
*   of a bodhisattva.*

THIS IS ESPECIALLY TRUE FOR LAMAS, senior monks, and important people who have a large circle of admirers who wish to show their respect and make many offerings. If we are in that position and spend our time being invited out and having lots of fuss made over us, it could promote our sense of arrogance and a love of comfort. Obviously, that is to be avoided. To make offerings and to show respect are positive acts from the side of the donor. We should always honor and respect lamas and teachers. But if the recipient begins to expect such attention and enjoys being the center of everybody's adoration, then they are in trouble.

Of course, Thogme Sangpo was an important lama in his day, so here he is warning his fellow lamas to watch out because some lamas spend all their time going out to perform household pujas and raking in the offerings. Then they are so busy that they forget what they are really supposed to be doing, which is studying, contemplating, and meditating. This is especially true if they are newly set out on the path, as that is when they should be spending their time studying and practicing. If they get drawn into going on the usual lama circuit then it can happen that their practice declines, and they start to expect people's respect and adoration, which is even worse.

This is really a big danger, especially in this present day when there are many young incarnate lamas—the rebirths of great lamas who had already set up so many Dharma centers all around the world in the past. These incarnations of great lamas are recognized within a very short time, and if they are not careful, they are sent around the globe because the Dharma centers need to make money and keep the students motivated and interested. These young teenage boys are sent out, and of course everyone adores them because they look so fresh and pretty. They are often cute, but they haven't done much cultivation in this lifetime. These former great lamas from Tibet not only had studied since the age of six but they often spent twenty to thirty years in retreat during their lifetime before they started to teach.

Nowadays everybody is in such a hurry, and the Dharma centers are not well established in the way that the monasteries were back in Tibet when they didn't really need the lama to be there physically. Sometimes the head lama would only emerge from retreat once or twice a year for important rituals or to give blessings. But nowadays these monasteries in exile rely on outside funding because they don't own the vast quantities of land and villages the way they used to. As a result, they send these young incarnate lamas all around the world before they are ready, when they are still not fully cooked; in fact, they are half baked. It is hard for them, too, since they know they are not ready. They haven't finished all their studies, and they haven't practiced much. Some of them haven't even done *ngondro*[56] and yet there they are, set up on a high throne like they are the Buddha himself. This is very dangerous not only for the students but also for the lamas because they have a huge responsibility, and they haven't even finished their training yet.

This verse, although it was written six hundred years ago, is actually even more relevant today when we have this whole new batch of "recycled" lamas coming out in this new fashionable edition. Many of them are brilliant, but because they are not properly trained and have not done nearly enough practice, all of the unquestioning adulation they receive could go to their head. There is a notion that is circulated that whatever a lama says must be true, even if it is nonsense. This is the antithesis of Dharma, which places a strong emphasis on critical intellect and analysis. It is dangerous to fall into this kind of belief and behavior, for the students but also for the so-called lama.

34

Giving Up Harsh Speech

Harsh words disturb the minds of others
And spoil our own bodhisattva practice.
Therefore, to give up rough speech,
Which others find unpleasant, is the practice
*   of a bodhisattva.*

WELL, THIS IS PRETTY OBVIOUS. We like people to speak kind words to us. We don't like them to speak hurtful, harmful, harsh words to us. Since we don't like it, and other people don't like it, we just don't do it.

Humans are the only beings on the planet that communicate through verbal languages, which brings us together but also divides us. Of course, other animals communicate, but they don't converse through the clumsiness of language. They have their own much more subtle way of interconnecting.

Because we have language, we are responsible for our speech. People can be more hurt by words than by physical brutality. In fact, verbal abuse can cause much more lasting harm. We say, "Sticks and stones may break my bones, but words can never harm me." The Tibetans more or less say, "Sticks and stones only break our bones, but harsh words can tear our heart to pieces." It is true, so we should put a guard on our tongue and be careful of what we say—and not just the words but the tone as well. Dilgo Khyentse Rinpoche says:

Most of the wars that devastate the world are started by harsh words. Quarrels, rancorous resentment, and endlessly perpetuated feuds all arise because tolerance and patience are lacking.[57]

Parents especially should be careful of what they say to their children because if they speak harshly to them, the children may carry that rebuke all their life. A lot of low self-esteem comes from early childhood, from something that the child heard from their parents who loved them but maybe were irritated at the time and spoke harshly. Many children are damaged from hearing abusive talk directed from parents toward themselves or from their parents to each other.

We should be careful with our speech. It should be truthful so people can trust that we are not cheating them, we are not telling anything that is not true, but at the same time our words should be kind and helpful, if possible. Sometimes we have to say things that seem unkind, but nonetheless, if they are intended to help, then we have to say them. But first we should check on our genuine motivation. Also we should not engage too much in a lot of garrulous chatter. Some people just babble away, saying aloud whatever is going through their head. This is just distraction. Who needs it? We should be conscious of our speech and the effect it has on others. Sometimes the highest speech is simply noble silence.

35

Cutting Negative Emotions

*When emotions become habitual, they are hard to get
    rid of with antidotes.
Therefore, with mindfulness and vigilance, to seize the
    weapon of the antidote
And crush attachment and other negative emotions
The moment they arise is the practice of a bodhisattva.*

THIS IS RATHER LIKE what we were dealing with earlier concerning anger. It is important to cultivate precise and clear mindfulness and the vigilance that oversees what we are doing and checks up on our state of mind. Here mindfulness means being clearly present and knowing what we are doing and thinking and feeling while we are doing it. Dilgo Khyentse Rinpoche notes the following in his commentary on this verse:

> When your mind is distracted, you can be bitten by a mosquito without your even noticing it. But when your mind is quiet, you will feel a mosquito bite straight away. In the same way, the mind needs to be relaxed and quiet if it is to become aware of its empty nature. The practice of shamatha is done for this reason, and through such practice even a person with strong emotions will gradually acquire self-control and inner calm. When the mind comes to a stable state of

relaxed concentration, your habitual tendencies fade away by themselves, while altruism and compassion naturally develop and expand. Eventually, you will come to a state of ease in the unceasing flow of the absolute nature.[58]

This vigilance doesn't need to remain all the time; it just looks in and checks. Is our mind distracted, is it sinking, is it full of negative thoughts? What's going on there? When it checks, if everything is running smoothly, then it recedes back and comes back later to check again. It ensures that the mind is doing what it should be doing.

The more precise our sense of presence is, the more conscious we are of what is happening in the moment, the more clear and vivid that becomes. Then we are able to catch these negative emotions like attachment and anger, jealousy and pride, and all the other negative emotions. If we can catch the afflictive emotion in the moment it arises and see it nakedly, it will dissolve and transform into sharp wisdom energy. This comes with habitual practice.

Usually if we are used to being angry when something upsets us, or we are used to being greedy every time we see something we like, or we get jealous every time somebody has something that we want, then we just get used to reacting like that. It becomes our neural pathway. Unless we are alert, it is difficult to apply the antidote once we are way down the road to expressing our afflictive emotions.

We need to develop mindfulness, a clarity of mind that rests in the moment and is conscious of these habitual negative emotions as soon as they arise, so we can zap them before they carry on gathering momentum and explode into their usual unskillful responses. The Buddha said that mindfulness is the path to liberation. Mindfulness means the quality of being present, of being aware, of knowing, which we need to cultivate in our daily life.

The Buddha started by saying first of all to be conscious of our physical movements. When standing know that you are standing.

When sitting know that you are sitting and so forth. Then bring that awareness to the feelings and sensations of pleasure, displeasure, and neutrality. Then bring that awareness to the mind—what is mind doing at this moment? And then also to the interaction between external phenomena and our mental input. The path of practice is the path of becoming more conscious, and the more conscious we become, the quicker we can deal with the negative emotions as they arise.

36

Being Mindful

In short, wherever I am, whatever I do,
To be continually mindful and alert,
Asking, "What is the state of my mind?"
And accomplishing the good of others is the
*   practice of a bodhisattva.*

THANK YOU, VENERABLE THOGME, it is exactly that. We have to *know* what is going on in our mind while it is going on and not just get engulfed and swept away by the flood of our thoughts and feelings. It is important to be continually mindful and alert, asking, *What is the state of my mind?* At the same time, we also need to accomplish good for others. Dilgo Khyentse Rinpoche instructs us to do the following:

> Every day, check to what extent you are applying the teach-ings, how often you are managing to control your mind, and how many times you are falling under the power of negative emotions. Examining your own progress in this way will help you to decrease your clinging to the ordinary concerns of this life, and to increase your confidence in the teachings.[59]

The matching verse from Langri Thangpa's *Eight Verses for Training the Mind* drives this idea home:

In all my actions may I watch my mind,
And as soon as disturbing emotions arise,
May I forcefully stop them at once,
Since they will hurt both me and others.[60]

When we are sitting in our meditation, if we are observing the mind, which is an excellent thing to do, we are just watching the thoughts streaming by, like the traditional example of someone sitting on the banks of the river just watching the water going by. We are not plunging into the river and being swept along, as we normally would be. Now we are sitting back on the banks. Dilgo Khyentse Rinpoche described it as sitting in a train and watching all the scenery go by. Beautiful countryside, ugly slums, whatever—we just observe it. We don't jump off the train to explore everything that is passing by. We are sitting in a train just observing what is passing by.

During our formal meditation, when we are sitting in our posture, we do not judge our thoughts. We do not discriminate between thoughts, labeling some good and some bad. All thoughts and feelings are just thoughts and feelings. They are just empty energy. They are not "me," they are not "mine." We recognize the totally impermanent nature of all our conceptual thinking. At the same time, we develop the quality of being mindful, of being aware and conscious of what is going on in the mind. How to be present. During the day, in postmeditation, outside our formal meditation when we are just letting things go by—as we go about all our activities—we should still be aware of our mind. We should observe the mind at all times or at least as often as we can remember to.

I often repeat this story about when I first started practicing with the yogis in our monastery. They suggested making a commitment to observe the mind three times in every hour. Each hour on three occasions simply look at what the mind is doing at that moment: what am I thinking, what am I feeling at this moment?

Then gradually as we begin to do that, as that ability to be mindful grows, we become more conscious, more awake, and more present, and ready during the day "as soon as disturbing emotions arise." Disturbing emotions are the *kleshas*, which are attachment, anger, ignorance, pride or conceit, and doubt. As soon as a negative emotion arises, any negative emotion that disturbs the mind, then we should immediately recognize and face it. We recognize the underlying feeling of the thought as anger or aversion, irritation, annoyance, or self-righteousness. Or there is greed or grasping, attachment and so forth, or whatever negative emotion is underpinning the thoughts. These feelings and thoughts create a lot of problems for us and for everybody else, so it is important that in all activities, we examine our mind.

Before doing anything, we should examine the underlying motivation, because as the Buddha said, "Karma is intention." It is not so much what we do but why we do it. To take an extreme example, consider a murderer who takes up a sharp knife or scalpel and plunges it in somebody's heart, and they die. The underlying motivation is hatred or jealousy, which caused him to want to kill this person. On the other hand, we have a highly skilled surgeon, who likewise takes up the scalpel and inserts it into the chest in order to carry out a heart operation. Unfortunately, it fails and the patient dies, but the motivation of the surgeon was very different from the murderer. The intention of the surgeon was to help and to cure the person, not to harm them and kill them. Essentially, although the action was the same, and the result was the same—the person died—the karmic results would be different because the intention was different. This is why when we are undertaking any action it is important for us to see as honestly as possible the underlying intention behind us performing this action of body or speech.

It isn't just the action performed or words that we speak, but how it is said or done and with what intention. That is what counts. Therefore, we should be careful of what is going on in our mind during the day because our thoughts will lead our speech and our actions. If we want our speech and actions to be pure and beneficial, then we should be careful that the underlying motivation is likewise pure and beneficial.

If we see that there is negativity in the mind, we should recognize it because it is from this negativity, the disturbing emotions, that we then act unskillfully and cause a lot of problems for ourselves and for others and make bad karma. In general, when we are not mindful, we mess up. We need to be conscious of what's going on in our mind. If our mind is genuinely harmless and benign, it is unlikely that we will act unskillfully to harm either ourselves or others. We usually blame others for our troubles, but really the problem lies within.

"May I firmly face them and avert them" means to recognize negative emotions and then mitigate them. First we have to look at our thoughts and emotions. When afflictive emotions of any kind arise, such as anger, greed, pride, jealousy, or fear, at that moment if we face them honestly, without reacting, we can recognize that emotion for what it is. In this way we can decide how to deal with it. Throughout all Buddhist schools there is an emphasis on how to deal with the five afflictive emotions at all levels. We can uproot, transform, or transcend these powerful forces that underlie so much of egoic existence. Therefore, first we have to recognize a negative emotion that has arisen. We have to face it. We can't pretend that it is not really a negative emotion. It *is* a negative emotion. Then, depending on our practice and the level of our skill, we deal with it.

For example, if we suddenly find ourselves feeling angry, then we could try replacing anger with forbearance and patient endurance or arouse compassion and loving-kindness. Or we could face that anger and transform it into its essential energetic nature called mirrorlike wisdom. Or, as Shantideva says, if we are really angry and we can't at that point change the anger into a more positive emotion, then we should act like a piece of wood and just not react. Breathing in, breathing out, and counting to ten. Later, we can read a book on how to deal with anger.

The point is that everybody has negative emotions. If we didn't have any negative emotions at all, that would mean that we were totally egoless. In which case we would be arhats, which is wonderful. But most people are not quite there yet. We all have faults. We all have problems. If it is not one thing, it is another.

Having negative emotions is not the problem. After all, if we didn't have them, we wouldn't need a path. But the point is to recognize our negative emotions and then apply the antidotes. As long as we are in denial that we have any problems and we delude ourselves into thinking that it is everybody else that is the problem, then nothing will change. We will become more and more habituated to our negative emotions and reactions. Once we recognize what the real problem is, we can get to work. Whatever our problem is, there is always a remedy for it. It is similar to when we are sick. If we are in denial that we are sick, then we just get worse. But if we discover what the actual cause of our problem is, then there is probably a good cure, provided that we take the medicine. This is why it is important to observe the mind throughout the day as much as possible in all our actions and recognize what the underlying habitual thoughts and feelings are. If they are negative, we need to recognize that and change them. If they are positive or neutral, then there is no problem.

We have to become more aware, more centered, more conscious, and more present and at the same time open our heart to the happiness and benefit of others. That should keep us going. People always complain that they have no time to practice. Well as long as we are breathing, we can practice.

Dilgo Khyentse Rinpoche beautifully describes the essence of the practice of a bodhisattva when he says the following:

The essence of the practice of a bodhisattva is to transcend self-clinging and dedicate yourself completely to serving others. It is a practice based on your mind, rather than on how your actions might appear externally. True generosity, therefore, is to have no clinging; true discipline to have no desire; and true patience to be without hatred. Bodhisattvas can even give away their kingdom, their life, or their spouse and children because they do not have the slightest inner feeling of poverty or need and are ready to fulfill others' needs unconditionally. It does not matter how your actions might seem to anyone else—no particular "compassionate" appearance is necessary. What you do need is a pure mind. For instance, sweet and pleasing words spoken without any intention of helping others are meaningless. Even birds can sing beautiful songs. Wild animals such as tigers behave in a loving way to their cubs, but theirs is a partial love mixed with attachment. It does not extend to all beings. A bodhisattva possesses impartial love for all beings.[61]

37

Dedicating on Behalf of Others

Dedicating to enlightenment
Through wisdom purified of the three concepts
All merit achieved by such endeavor,
To remove the suffering of numberless beings, is the
  practice of a bodhisattva.

THE FIRST TWO LINES of this final verse mean that we dedicate the virtue without grasping at the notion that there is anyone who has dedicated the virtue, that there's anyone to dedicate it to, or there is any dedication going on. The second two lines indicate why we dedicate this merit—so that all sentient beings will be free of suffering. Amen.

Dilgo Khyentse Rinpoche explains how to dedicate merit in the following passage:

To dedicate merit in the best possible way—a way entirely free from the three concepts of a subject, an object, and an action—is possible only for someone who has fully realized emptiness. How, then, should we ordinary beings dedicate the merit, incapable as we are of such perfect dedication? We can do it by following in the footsteps of those who have that realization. The bodhisattva Samantabhadra mastered the ocean-like infinitude of a bodhisattva's aspirations, while Manjushri and Avalokiteshvara mastered the ocean-like infinitude of a bodhisattva's activity to benefit beings. When you dedicate merit, do it with the idea of emulating the way these great bodhisattvas dedicated merit, and use the perfect verses spoken by the Buddha or his followers who realized the ultimate, empty nature of everything. It gives your prayers much more power and efficacy.[62]

The Thirty-Seven Verses on the Practice of a Bodhisattva by Thogme Sangpo concludes as follows:

Following the teachings of the holy beings,
I have arranged the points taught in the sutras, tantra, and
     shastras
As *The Thirty-Seven Verses on the Practice of a Bodhisattva*
For the benefit of those who wish to train on the
     bodhisattva path.

Since my understanding is poor, and I have little education,
This is no composition to delight the learned;
But as it is based on the sutras and teachings of holy beings
I think it is genuinely the practice of the bodhisattvas.

However, it is hard for someone unintelligent like me
To fathom the great waves of the bodhisattvas' activities,
So I beg the forgiveness of the holy ones
For my contradictions, irrelevances, and other mistakes.

Through the merit arising from this
And through the power of the sublime bodhichitta, relative
     and absolute,
May all beings become like the Lord Avalokiteshvara,
Who is beyond the extremes of samsara and nirvana.[63]

—For his own benefit and that of others, Thogme, a teacher of scripture and logic, composed this text at Rinchen Phug, in Ngulchu.

Many lamas have expounded on this beautiful text with excellent commentaries. If you are interested, please really study these books and try to apply the principles to daily life because it is such a practical text. Apart from the book currently in your hands, a very good place to start is the commentary by Dilgo Khyentse Rinpoche released under the title *The Heart of Compassion*. There is also a recent translation of a widely regarded commentary on the practices by Ngawang Tenzin Norbu titled *A Guide to the Thirty-Seven Practices of a Bodhisattva*. There are also online resources such as videos of teachings by His Holiness the Dalai Lama.

Sometimes when we read books on profound philosophy or advanced meditation such as Mahamudra and Dzogchen, it all seems difficult unless we have endless amounts of time. We wonder how we will be able to accomplish such heights. But this text was written for daily life and daily practice, so there is no excuse not to read these verses, think about them, and apply them to our lives. We must become accustomed to these principles by applying them daily and being grateful for the opportunities our lives give us to actually put these values into practice by bringing the stuff of everyday life onto the path.

To close, I would like to share a quote from Ngawang Tenzin Norbu (1867–1940), a Nyingma master known for his own influential commentary of the *Thirty-Seven Verses*:

> In this realm of samsara, all of the suffering there is, without exception, arises from self-cherishing due to wishing for one's own happiness. Whatever mundane or transcendent happiness and benefit there is—such as the ultimate happiness on the level of a perfect Buddha—all of it is born from the intention to benefit and cherish others.[64]

Now it is your time to practice. Please contemplate what you have read in this book and apply the teachings in your daily life. In this way you are not only benefiting yourself, leading yourself to ultimate liberation, you are also actively cherishing others. In taming the mind and opening the heart, you are making yourself someone who is much more able to show compassion and kindness to all beings. If you diligently apply these teachings, you will eventually become a bodhisattva, a hero of boundless love and limitless compassion. What more could you want?

NOTES

1. Dilgo Khyentse, *The Heart of Compassion: The Thirty-Seven Verses on the Practice of a Bodhisattva* (Boulder: Shambhala, 2007), 49.

2. Khyentse, *Heart of Compassion*, 49.

3. Khyentse, *Heart of Compassion*, 45.

4. Khyentse, *Heart of Compassion*, 51.

5. Excerpt found in Khyentse, *Heart of Compassion*, 57.

6. Khyentse, *Heart of Compassion*, 55.

7. Jetsunma was in retreat in an isolated mountain cave in Lahaul, in Northern India, for twelve years. See Vicki Mackenzie's biography of Jetsunma titled *Cave in the Snow*.

8. Khyentse, *Heart of Compassion*, 54.

9. Khyentse, *Heart of Compassion*, 59.

10. Khyentse, *Heart of Compassion*, 61.

11. Khyentse, *Heart of Compassion*, 63–64.

12. Khyentse, *Heart of Compassion*, 68.

13. Khyentse, *Heart of Compassion*, 70.

14. Khyentse, *Heart of Compassion*, 73.

15. Khyentse, *Heart of Compassion*, 73.

16. Khyentse, *Heart of Compassion*, 73.

17. Khyentse, *Heart of Compassion*, 79.

18. Khyentse, *Heart of Compassion*, 79.

19. Khyentse, *Heart of Compassion*, 87.

20. Khyentse, *Heart of Compassion*, 84–85.

21. Khyentse, *Heart of Compassion*, 85.

22. Khyentse, *Heart of Compassion*, 91.

23. Geshe Sonam Rinchen, *Eight Verses for Training the Mind*, trans. Ruth Sonam (Boulder: Snow Lion, 2001), 00.

24. Rinchen, *Eight Verses for Training the Mind*, 69.

25. Khyentse, *Heart of Compassion*, 104.

26. Khyentse, *Heart of Compassion*, 110.

27. Rinchen, *Eight Verses for Training the Mind*, 53.

28. Khyentse, *Heart of Compassion*, 110.

29. Khyentse, *Heart of Compassion*, 112.

30. Rinchen, *Eight Verses for Training the Mind*, 57.

31. Khyentse, *Heart of Compassion*, 112.

32. Khyentse, *Heart of Compassion*, 116.

33. Rinchen, *Eight Verses for Training the Mind*, 63.

34. Khyentse, *Heart of Compassion*, 116–17.

35. Rinchen, *Eight Verses for Training the Mind*, 40.

36. Khyentse, *Heart of Compassion*, 117.

37. Khyentse, *Heart of Compassion*, 119.

38. Khyentse, *Heart of Compassion*, 121.

39. Khyentse, *Heart of Compassion*, 132.

40. Khyentse, *Heart of Compassion*, 124.

41. Khyentse, *Heart of Compassion*, 125–26.

42. Khyentse, *Heart of Compassion*, 133.

43. Khyentse, *Heart of Compassion*, 135–36.

44. Khyentse, *Heart of Compassion*, 147.

45. Rinchen, *Eight Verses for Training the Mind*, 73.

46. Khyentse, *Heart of Compassion*, 151.

47. Khyentse, *Heart of Compassion*, 138.

48. Khyentse, *Heart of Compassion*, 137.

49. Khyentse, *Heart of Compassion*, 139.

50. Khyentse, *Heart of Compassion*, 140.

51. Khyentse, *Heart of Compassion*, 143.

52. Khyentse, *Heart of Compassion*, 145.

53. Khyentse, *Heart of Compassion*, 148.

54. Khyentse, *Heart of Compassion*, 155.

55. Khyentse, *Heart of Compassion*, 157–58.

56. *Ngondro* is a set of preliminary practices, generally consisting of one hundred thousand repetitions of going for refuge, bodhichitta aspiration, mandala offering, *Vajrasattva*, and guru yoga practice.

57. Khyentse, *Heart of Compassion*, 165.

58. Khyentse, *Heart of Compassion*, 169.

59. Khyentse, *Heart of Compassion*, 170–71.

60. Rinchen, *Eight Verses for Training the Mind*, 45.

61. Khyentse, *Heart of Compassion*, 191–92.

62. Khyentse, *Heart of Compassion*, 174.

63. Khyentse, *Heart of Compassion*, 37.

64. Ngawang Tenzin Norbu, *A Guide to the Thirty-Seven Practices of a Bodhisattva* (Boulder: Snow Lion, 2020), 85.

SUGGESTED FURTHER READING

Mackenzie, Vicki. *Cave in the Snow: A Western Woman's Quest for Enlightenment*. New York: Bloomsbury, 1998.

Palmo, Jetsunma Tenzin. *Into the Heart of Life*. Boulder: Shambhala, 2011.

————. *Reflections on a Mountain Lake: Teachings on Practical Buddhism*. Boulder: Snow Lion, 2002.

————. *Three Teachings*. Australia: Buddha Dharma Education Association, 2000.

Books on Lojong

Khyentse Rinpoche, Dilgo. *Enlightened Courage: An Explanation of the Seven-Point Mind Training*. Translated by Padmakara Translation Group. Boulder: Shambhala, 2006.

————. *The Heart of Compassion: The Thirty-Seven Verses on the Practice of a Bodhisattva*. Translated by Padmakara Translation Group. Boulder: Shambhala, 2007.

Norbu, Ngawang Tenzin. *A Guide to the Thirty-Seven Practices of a Bodhisattva*. Translated by Christopher Stagg. Boulder: Shambhala, 2020.

Image by Sol Voron, taken in
Australia, April 2008.

ABOUT THE AUTHOR

Jetsunma Tenzin Palmo, born in England in 1943, is a fully ordained nun (*bhikshuni*) in the Drukpa lineage of the Kagyu school of Tibetan Buddhism. She is an author, teacher, and founder of the Dongyu Gatsal Ling Nunnery in Himachal Pradesh, India. Jetsunma is renowned for being one of the few Western-born practitioners fully trained in the East, having spent twelve years living in a remote cave in the Himalayas, three of those years in strict meditation retreat. Jetsunma's heart teacher was the Eighth Khamtrul Rinpoche, Dongyu Nyima (1931–1980), who reestablished the Khampagar lineage and monastery in Northern India after the destruction of the original during the Chinese invasion and occupation of Tibet. The title of Jetsunma (revered lady) was bestowed on her by the head of the Drukpa lineage, the Twelfth Gyalwang Drukpa, in recognition of her spiritual achievements as a nun and her efforts in promoting the status of female practitioners in Tibetan Buddhism. No other Westerner has been formally granted a title of such high esteem.